PREACHING That Speaks to WOMEN

PREACHING That Speaks to WOMEN

ALICE P. MATHEWS

Foreword by Haddon W. Robinson

Published by Baker Academic
a division of Baker Book House Company
P.O. Box 6287, Grand Rapids, MI 49516-6287
www.bakeracademic.com

and

Inter-Varsity Press
38 De Montfort Street
Leicester LE1 7GP
England
Email: ivp@uccf.org.uk
Web site: www.ivpbooks.com

Printed in the United States of America

Library of Congress Cataloging-in-Publication Data

Mathews, Alice P., 1930–
Preaching that speaks to women / Alice P. Mathews ; foreword by Haddon W. Robinson.
p. cm.
Includes bibliographical references and index.
ISBN 0-8010-2367-X (pbk.)
1. Preaching to women. 2. Communication—Religious aspects—Christianity.
I. Title.
BV4235.W65M38 2003
251′.0082—dc21 2002026198

British Library Cataloguing in Publication Data
A catalogue record for this book is available from the British Library.
Inter-Varsity Press ISBN 0-85111-990-5

Contents

Foreword

Garrison Keillor describes a Lutheran ushering Olympics contest that he maintains takes place annually in Orlando, Florida. The competition pits teams against one another to see which ushers can best seat 150 Unitarians in a Lutheran church service and keep them there to the end without any sneaking out the back.

Some preachers compete in another Olympic contest. They test how long they can keep women in the church pews while ignoring them completely. It is a dangerous sport, and the "winners" may end up losers. In virtually every congregation, 60 percent or more of regular attendees are women, but many male preachers seldom refer to them or use illustrations or applications specifically related to their experiences. The fact that these women are willing to listen to sermons as unrelated to them as Lutheran liturgy is to Unitarians says something noble about the patience of women.

Sermons are not addressed to "Occupant" or "To Whom It May Concern." Sermons have particular people in mind. They are preached at 11:20 A.M. to the people assembled at the church located at Fifth and Main. Effective preachers know their Bibles, and they know their particular audience. Usually ministers zero in on the characteristics of different age groups. I have file folders crammed with descriptions of Busters, Boomers, Builders, and Generations X, Y, and Z that slice up the culture like a cadaver. Most of these analyses produced for church leaders take women for granted. In some congregations, the only consideration given to women is whether or not they can be ordained.

Yet women have made their mark on our society. They head up large corporations. They fly jets, and they win public office. They teach our children and hold prestigious chairs in great universities. They serve as physicians and dentists. They mother our children and do so at times under overwhelming adversity. Without women, churches would have trouble operating, and the missionary corps would be depleted. The women who sit before us are not our grandmothers' generation. In the past, women may have come to church out of loyalty to the pastor or to the institution, but their granddaughters want more. They want to be treated as Christians who possess all the Spirit's gifts and not as second-rate citizens of the kingdom. If we Christian leaders ignore them, we do so to our peril and theirs.

Alice Mathews is qualified to write about women and how to communicate to them. She knows the territory. She has earned a Ph.D. in women's studies, but she does not suffer from a celibacy of the intellect. She has exercised her gifts as a pastor's wife, a missionary, a seminary dean, an author, a teacher, a conference speaker, and an office worker. She has also served her time as a listener in the pew. She writes about women as listeners because she knows them, and those who know her know she loves and values them.

Reading what she has written will help you to address effectively both halves of the human race.

Haddon W. Robinson

Acknowledgments

I was brought up to pay my honest debts. It was right to "keep short accounts" or, in the words of Scripture, to "owe no one anything, except to love one another" (Rom. 13:8 NRSV). What I have discovered in later years is that such a policy is wise where money is concerned but that there are other kinds of debts that can never be repaid. I cannot adequately repay the people who have placed a thumbprint on my mind and my life. All I can do at this point is acknowledge my debts to them.

This book is about the intersection of two subjects: gender and preaching. The friends who have helped me find a path through the gender minefield include Paula Nesbitt, Gay Hubbard, and Maria Boccia—three women of amazing intellect who never fail to challenge me when I tend toward cliches or am ready to settle for unexamined dichotomies. Behind them stands an unseen chorus of hundreds of women with whom I have interacted in church and parachurch settings over the past three decades in ministry to women. They have provided the ongoing empirical test group for the ideas in this book.

This book is also about preaching. One person towers above all others as the primary influence on my thinking about preaching. That person, of course, is Haddon Robinson. It was in auditing some of his courses in the early 1980s that I began to understand the magnitude of the preaching task. It was he who forced me to think about the intersection of preaching and gender in the late 1980s when he asked me to talk to his Doctor of Ministry students about women as listeners. It has been in the ongoing radio work with him and Mart DeHaan for *Discover the Word* that I have learned to practice some of the basic principles of communication theory that lie behind the preaching task. More recently, it was the opportunity to work with him on the revision of *Biblical Preaching* that finally helped me to nail down some things about preaching in my mind.

That I owe these debts to Paula, Gay, Maria, and Haddon is unquestionable. That I have even begun to repay these debts in this book is a separate question. I take full responsibility for what I have done (or have failed to do) with the ideas they have supplied to me over the years.

There is one more unpayable debt. It is to Randall, my companion in life for more than half a century. I cannot count the times he patiently answered the phone for me while I pounded away on this book up in our loft. Or the many breakfasts he prepared, the dishes he washed, or the floors he vacuumed. When I thank him, he reminds me of all the times I did those things for him so that he could do his work. And we both smile and acknowledge the glory of an enduring marriage bound by the strong cords of love. But the debt remains. And that is a good thing. There are times when it is not wise to keep short accounts.

Introduction

It is a myth that writers stand outside what they write, objectively uninvolved except in a most cerebral way. One thing the study of hermeneutics makes clear is that we choose subjects and shape our discussion of those subjects based on our own past and present struggles and questions. Because I as a reader want to know about some of the struggles and questions faced by the authors I read, I think it is only fair that I introduce this book with a brief description of my own journey.

As a child I was intrigued by the art of preaching. I certainly had plenty of exposure to all kinds! Not only did I listen to our pastor preach every Sunday morning and Sunday evening, but I also listened to almost all of the good (and some mediocre) evangelists and Bible teachers in North America over the years. Our church sponsored six weeks of evangelistic tent meetings every summer with a procession of speakers, and our family never missed a single evening session. When the tent meetings ended, we were bundled into the car and taken to a Bible conference in western Michigan for two more weeks of preaching—morning and evening. Some preachers captured and held my rapt attention. As others preached, I was more intent on catching crickets leaping about on the wood-chip floor. What made the difference?

I grew up in an era in which making wisecracks about women was fairly standard preaching fare, good for a few laughs. This made me uncomfortable because I was female, growing toward womanhood. It was later in a Christian college that I became aware of gender bias. The professor would ask a question to which I was sure I had a good answer. But my hand in the air was frequently ignored as the professor waited for a fellow in the class to venture a guess. During four years of college I had only one female professor. The realization grew that I would have to be cautious in what was clearly a man's world.

Virtually nothing that happened to me in the next twenty years dispelled that realization. During the years my husband spent as a seminary student and a pastor, and during our years on the mission field, I encountered very few men who included me in conversations or listened when I spoke. Yes, it was a man's world. For those twenty years I buried myself in two great passions: domesticity and youth ministry. With four growing children and an open parsonage, and with responsibilities for groups of high school and college students in our churches or overseas, I had my hands full. These were good years, happy years, but years tinged by what I felt was a lack of respect for my personhood on the part of the men I encountered.

In 1970, two women invited me to join them in beginning an innovative outreach ministry to women in Paris, France, where we were working. That was a turning point in my life as I "discovered" women. It seems strange to say that, having at that point been a girl, then a woman for forty years. As I shifted from youth ministries to women's ministries, I began listening to women with different ears. What I heard set my feet on a new path: If I was called to teach God's Word relevantly to women, I needed to know much more about their realities. So in addition to my ongoing study of the Scriptures, I began to study the problems women faced in society and the issues communicators had to confront in order to minister effectively to women.

That second line of study sent me back to school for a Ph.D. in religion and social change as I sought to understand what women needed to hear from God's Word in order to evaluate and deal with what they were hearing from the contemporary culture. By then, we had returned to the United States after seventeen years of ministry in Europe, and I had settled into women's ministries in churches and in a seminary setting. I have to admit that I was reluctant at first to join a seminary staff because my experiences with Christian men had been overwhelmingly negative in the past. But God knew my need and at Denver Seminary gave me strong support from a number of men on the faculty (Donald

Burdick, Ralph Covell, William Thomas, and Haddon Robinson, among others). My time there began the process of healing a hurt I had often prayed about but felt powerless to deal with myself.

It was also at Denver Seminary that I began to think constructively about the intersection of gender and preaching. (It is impossible to work closely with Haddon Robinson for over two decades and *not* think a great deal about preaching!) I was invited to talk about that intersection, then to write about it, and eventually to teach courses on it. I also made it a major emphasis in my doctoral studies. I do not pretend to know everything about the subject. This book, therefore, is a kind of work in progress. But if my journey has brought together in these pages something that can help others communicate more effectively to women for the glory of God, then I am well rewarded for taking the risk of writing it.

The book is organized broadly on the way in which Scripture calls us to love God—with all our hearts, souls, minds, and strength—and our neighbors as ourselves (Lev. 19:18; Deut. 6:4; Matt. 22:37–40; Luke 10:27). Chapter 1 introduces the subject of the book by exploring both the myths and the legitimate parameters for speaking about women as listeners. Much that has been written about how men and women are different from one another does not stand up to responsible analysis. Chapter 1 attempts to lay out some general principles for what can and cannot be said about women and men, based on social science and physical science evidence. Throughout the book the myths and the legitimate facts will be laid alongside Scripture in an effort to evaluate them not merely through a scientific lens but also through the lens of the Bible.

Chapter 2 introduces the first way we as Christians are called to love God: with all our hearts. Some commentators tell us that loving God with a whole heart means loving God with our will, the seat of volition and the moral life. The chapter explores ethical decision-making—how men and women may differ in this critical area and how preachers can reach both women and men as they preach on moral issues.

Chapter 3 moves to loving God with all our souls. The word *soul* is interpreted in this chapter in light of the Hebrew use of the word as the vital life principle in contrast to inert dust, not in the philosophical Greek sense of an immortal entity. The soul carries a psychophysical sense of the self giving life to the body. The New Testament uses the Greek word *psychē* to translate the Hebrew word, with the sense of loving God with the vital psychological part of our being. The chapter explores women's psychology—responses to stress, issues of low self-esteem, and women's heightened susceptibility to depression. It then examines how preaching can bring women to psychological wholeness so that they can love God with all their souls.

Chapters 4, 5, and 6 focus on loving God with all our minds. Chapters 4 and 5 examine various epistemologies that hinder or help women to love God with their minds. Chapter 6 looks specifically at the connection between epistemology and spirituality and how preachers can help women overcome various barriers to love God with their minds.

Chapters 7 and 8 focus on loving God with all our strength—with all the abilities and gifts God has given to each of us. Chapter 7 explores issues of power and powerlessness for women, and chapter 8 examines how women lead and the kind of leadership a preacher can employ to guide listeners to the full use of their abilities in the service of God's kingdom.

Chapter 9 focuses on loving our neighbors as we love ourselves. It looks at women who often feel marginalized by the church and challenges preachers to motivate listeners to embrace those who are different from themselves.

Finally, chapter 10 examines some common communication gaffes in speaking to women and calls preachers to greater sensitivity to the women in their congregations.

Writing a book means leaving out at least as much as is included. It is not easy to know what to omit. For that reason, I have put a great deal of material into notes that started out in the body of the first draft. I have also left much material on the cutting-room floor. For those readers who want to pursue individual topics further, the notes offer suggested reading in a number of areas.

At the time of this writing, I am teaching courses in women's ministries at Gordon-Conwell Theological Seminary. In class I tell lots of stories about individual women's struggles and hurts. If you have worked with women or listened to them for very long, you can probably tell many stories yourself. The stories remind all of us of the gap between God's ideal for each of us and our reality in a fallen world. My prayer is that this book will enable preachers to close that gap a bit more as they deepen their understanding of women as listeners.

1

Is It True That Men Are from Mars and Women Are from Venus?

In the lighthearted film *What Women Want,* Mel Gibson's character accidentally receives the ability to hear audibly the unspoken thoughts of women around him. As a ruthless and chauvinistic advertising man, he starts out using this astonishing new resource against the women in his professional life. But as time goes on, he finds that women's unspoken thoughts begin to shape his own way of thinking—and his ability to communicate more effectively with women.

Mel Gibson's character was "a man's man." He knew the "male" way to think and act, and he displayed a contempt for anything that differed from that. So the sudden ability to get inside women's heads shook him up. Much of what he had thought or assumed about women turned out to be inaccurate. Only when he began to "hear" their unspoken thoughts was he forced to revise his assumptions about women.

Most of us go through life with sets of assumptions about gender that are largely based on myth. This is the stuff of comedy—on the stage, in television sitcoms, or in films such as *What Women Want.* These assumptions are usually not as funny when played out in real living rooms or bedrooms. And it is not funny at all when these myth-based assumptions inform sermons that deal with matters of life and death for both men and women.

This book is about the myths and the realities surrounding the lives of women sitting in church pews week after week. And it is about the ways in which these myths and realities determine the messages women hear from the pulpit. Most importantly, this book is about the ways that pastors can preach so that women can hear God's truth plainly and convincingly and incorporate it into their lives.

When a preacher's assumptions about women correspond closely to the reality of women's lives, it is far more likely that the message women receive from the pulpit will speak with power and conviction to the issues of their lives and the needs of their hearts. Unlike Mel Gibson's character, however, pastors cannot hear audibly the unspoken thoughts of women. How, then, can a pastor gain reliable clues to the messages women are actually receiving from the pulpit?

Take a moment to step out of your skin mentally. Close your eyes and imagine that you wake up tomorrow morning and almost immediately know that something is "wrong." Your body has changed as you slept. If you went to bed as a man, you wake up as a woman. If you went to bed as a woman, you wake up as a man.[1]

First, there is the shock of discovering that you have to deal with many routine habits in a different way. You use the bathroom differently. You struggle to put on very different clothes. You may have to deal with whiskers that grew during the night: How does a former woman deal with shaving? Or how does a former man manage a bad hair day, having no prior experience with curling irons or hot rollers? That's the initial shock.

But the real shock steals over you as you begin to discover what this mysterious change means for your work life and your home life. You discover that as a result of this change you understand differently what it is to be a man or to be a woman. And you find yourself with a different attitude toward half the human race. Your expectations for those around you who are different from you have changed. Perhaps uncomfortably, you discover that their expectations for you have changed as well. These expectations define in new ways what you can and cannot do. You may quickly discover that you are expected to perform in areas that were previously unfamiliar to you or that now, disappointingly, you are prohibited from participating in activities that fascinate you or in relationships you once found satisfying. The "idyllic" existence you once believed the other half of the human race enjoyed has now been reduced to the drudgery of daily responsibilities. As you move through the day, you find yourself confronted with beliefs and expectations that leave you uncertain, socially disoriented, and subtly at odds with yourself and others.[2]

You may wonder why you should bother with such an improbable test of your imagination. Folk wisdom tells us that we cannot understand another person's problems or life until we have walked a mile in that person's shoes. And while that is usually not an option for us, there are lesser ways in which we can *virtually* walk that mile. Losing a game of Monopoly is not the same as losing your life savings in the real estate market. But the game can, nevertheless, help you grasp some of the principles behind the risks.

This book is designed to help you (if you are a male reader)[3] to step virtually into the skin of a woman, to listen as she listens, to hear what she hears, and to think as she might think—about God, the Bible, and the Christian life. If you are a preacher, this book can help you shape your sermons and your delivery in ways that connect more profoundly with women's experiences. It may also enable you to avoid common pitfalls in preaching that can obscure the truths of the gospel for many women. In short, as you stand before your congregation each week, you may find that applying the insights in this book will radically change your pulpit ministry. That could be good news for women in the pews.

Those of us who have worked closely with Haddon Robinson over the years have often heard him describe the difference between amateur and professional or skilled speakers in this way: An amateur speaker usually leads off with the question "What should I talk about?" The skilled speaker starts with the question "Who is my audience?" Before you can decide on a topic, you need to know whether you are being asked to talk to a group of teens, a group of business people, or a group of senior citizens. In such groups, the differences in interests, attitudes, and even vocabularies are somewhat self-evident.

Less self-evident are the possible differences in interests, attitudes, and even vocabularies between a group of men, a group of women, and a mixed audience. Consequently, the tendency in preaching is to think that where gender is concerned, one size fits all. Unfortunately, failure to recognize powerful social differences between women and men can result in failure to communicate truth at a level that reaches people's lives.

When I was a child growing up in Detroit, Michigan, during the 1930s and 1940s, my parents were active in a rapidly growing church near our house. During the nine-year ministry of a dynamic pastor, the congregation grew from fewer than 250 to more than 1,400 during the Great Depression and the Second World War. Yet even as a child, I was miffed each time I heard the pastor boast from the pulpit that he did not have to make an effort to bring in women and children; he simply focused on the men. He was sure that if he had the men, he would have the wives and kids as well. That was in the 1930s and 1940s, and he was probably right. On Sunday mornings he taught a men's Bible class of four hundred men in an abandoned bank building across the street from the church, and he got not only those men but also their families. The unusual growth of the church seemed to bear out his basic church-growth philosophy.

Would that pastor have the same success in the twenty-first century? Almost certainly not. The world has changed dramatically in the last fifty years. I think of the surprising range of change in my own life. Some of the messages I heard as a young girl would chase me out the door today. However nostalgic some people may be about the simpler certitudes of that earlier day, those certitudes have been eroded. The world in which we now seek to speak the good news of the gospel has been shaped by a succession of wars, the civil rights and women's movements, the shift from an industrial to a technological society, and the impact of postmodern questions and answers in the wider world of media, politics, and education. Today the answer to the question "Who is my audience?" is far more complex than most speakers think when both women and men are part of that audience.

When we talk about an audience, however, we also talk about its context. A talk-show audience is not the same as a Sunday morning congregation. Nor is a staid congregation in a formal church the same as an audience in a less formal megachurch. The social context of an audience is as important as the makeup of the audience itself. Furthermore, in a single church with similar people in the pews, the audience can be different depending on the personality, beliefs, or attitudes of the speaker. Listeners who may be open to new insights from one speaker may reject those same insights when spoken by a different preacher. The pastor is also part of the context that shapes listeners' responses.

What are the messages the average woman may hear when she attends church on Sunday? She *may* hear the messages contained in the pastor's words. She may hear other messages in what the pastor does *not* say. She is likely to pick up nonverbal messages from the preacher's stance in the pulpit. She may receive unintended messages from the informal social interactions that occur before or after the service. But whatever the messages she receives, the way in which the contemporary woman hears is likely to be vastly different from my mother's way of hearing in the 1930s.

In subtle ways, preaching to women is not the same as preaching to men. When the pastor steps into the pulpit on a Sunday morning, the challenge of speaking God's Word effectively to *all* the people may be greater than the preacher realizes. In *Telling the Truth*, Frederick Buechner describes a typical audience:

> In the front row the old ladies turn up their hearing aids, and a young lady slips her six year old a Lifesaver and a Magic Marker. A college sophomore home on vacation, who is there because he was dragged there, slumps forward with his chin in his hand. The vice-president of a bank who twice that week has seriously contemplated suicide places his hymnal in the rack. A pregnant girl feels the life stir within her. A high school math teacher, who for twenty years has managed to keep his homosexuality a secret for the most part even from himself, creases his order of service down the center with his thumbnail and tucks it under his knee.

Buechner then goes on to describe the preacher:

> The preacher pulls the little cord that turns on the lectern light and deals out his note cards like a riverboat gambler. The stakes have never been higher. Two minutes from now he may have lost his listeners completely to their own thoughts, but at this moment he has them in the palm of his hand. The silence in the shabby church is deafening because everybody is listening to it. Everybody is listening, even himself. Everybody knows the kind of things he has told them before and has not told them, but who knows what this time he will tell them, out of the silence he will tell them? Let him tell them the truth.[4]

That is your privilege. That is your challenge.

Is It Really True That Men Are from Mars and Women Are from Venus?

In the 1990s, John Gray made at least a small fortune with his book *Men Are from Mars, Women Are from Venus*. The book was on best-seller lists for years and was discussed on almost every talk show. It also fed some of the prevailing myths about women and men. Was that book on target? Are men and women from different planets?

When we look at some of the recent popular literature, we may conclude that John Gray was right. Both Christian and secular writers appear to have accepted his basic premise. For example, in *Men and Masculinity,* British evangelical leader Roy McCloughry concluded that "all conversation between men and women is cross-cultural conversation."[5] He later elaborated by quoting Deborah Tannen's *You Just Don't Understand: Men and Women in Conversation.* Tannen makes the point that men and women use conversation for different purposes: Women use conversation to seek confirmation, to make connections, and to reinforce intimacy; men, on the other hand, use conversation primarily to protect their independence and to negotiate status.[6]

If, in fact, there is truth in these conclusions, the task of preaching to mixed audiences may be far more complicated than most preachers know. It is possible that the way a doctrine is taught or an illustration is selected can actually backfire on half (or more) of an audience, simply because we think that men and women hear the words we have spoken in the same way. Is it possible that men and women in the same country, in the same town, in the same church could actually move within different cultures, as the opening exercise may have shown us? If it *is* true, what are the implications for the preaching task?

Anthropologist and missiologist Paul Hiebert discusses culture as the way in which ideas, feelings, and values are shared by a group of people.[7] In normal use, the word *culture* refers to any group's "way of life"—how people act based on what they believe, feel, and value. Churches have their own cultures—their shared beliefs, feelings, and values. Ethnic groups have their own cultures—their shared beliefs, feelings, and values. Nations have their own cultures—their shared beliefs, feelings, and values. It may be that men and women in North America have subtly different cultures, with somewhat different sets of shared beliefs, feelings, and values.

We tend to think that "all Americans" or "all Methodists" (or Baptists or Pentecostals or whatever) would hear messages in similar ways. Yet it takes only a few minutes of reflection to recognize that deep divisions exist even within our ethnic or denominational subcultures. That should alert us to the possibility that men and women may actually live in different worlds of ideas, feelings, and values.[8]

Historian Anne Firor Scott tells us that our culture grinds the lens through which we view reality.[9] A lens that allows us to see one thing clearly may also make other things fuzzy, impossible to see. Anyone who wears bifocals understands how that works: A near-sighted person needs one lens for reading and a separate lens for seeing anything more than a few feet away. Is it possible that men and women have different cultural "lenses" that cause them to look at reality in differing ways?

- Our culture shapes our *ideas*, our cultural knowledge.[10] Cultural knowledge is not only the categories we use to sort out reality but also the assumptions and beliefs we have about reality—the nature of the world around us and how it works. Our culture provides us with the basic building blocks of our thoughts, so we must ask if there is a separate male culture that provides men with ingredients for their thoughts that are different from those provided to women. Perhaps no. Perhaps yes. But it is a question we must ask.
- Our culture shapes our *feelings* about things—our attitudes, our notions of what is beautiful or ugly, our tastes in food and dress, how we like to enjoy life, how we experience sorrow or joy. Clearly, women have cultural permission to feel and express emotion in ways different from those of men.
- Our culture shapes our *values,* which help us judge which things are moral and which are immoral. Many women would assert that men have a different moral code with its own culturally defined sins—not identical to the moral code that defines sin for women. Men and women do not always agree on which acts are righteous and which are immoral.

It may be easier for us to grasp the reality of cultural difference in terms of different generations. When I am with any of my six grandsons, I hear them speak a language different from my own. Yes, they use words that are in my vocabulary—words such as *cool* or *awesome* or *radical*—but they do not attach the same meanings to them. So I might ask Chris, "When you say that Eric is *cool,* what do you mean? What's *cool* about Eric? He seems pretty warm to me." I listen to the vast array of inflections used in the ways my grandsons pronounce a word such as *cool,* and I know that it is an important word with many meanings and many uses. I just don't speak that language.

But if my husband, Randall, and I sit sipping coffee together after breakfast, chatting about our family, our work, and the day ahead of us, I can easily assume that he and I speak the same language. After all, we have lived together for more than half a century! But once in a while he says something that reminds me that we are *not* always speaking the same language. For example, though we both grew up during the Great Depression and share conservative attitudes about the way we use money, we do not talk about money in the same way. His father lost his job in 1933 and was unable to support the family. My father had work throughout the Depression, and though we were poor by today's standards, we never went hungry. As a result, I tend not to worry about losing everything we have in the same way Randall does. He is more cautious about spending than I am, coming out of a life experience that is different from mine. Thus, the words *save* and *spend* carry different freight for him.[11]

The same thing happens countless times between the pulpit and the pew. When a pastor steps into the pulpit on Sunday morning, the odds make it likely that nearly three out of every four adults waiting to hear the sermon are women, although the ratio will vary from church to church. But the reality is that most pastors speak to more women than men every Sunday. It is this reality that makes it practical and logical to think about women as listeners:

- What kind of word from God do you think today's woman may be listening for?
- What kind of word from God do you think she might be *hearing,* regardless of what you are saying?
- What preoccupations does she have that you must break through?
- Does she differ from men in the audience in significant ways?
- If so, what are the implications for your preaching each week?

The purpose of this book is to help you find adequate and helpful answers to those questions. To do so, we will explore together relevant aspects of the sociology of gender, women's psychology, how women know what they know, and how they make their moral decisions. In the process, we will examine whether there is any solid evidence for cultural differences between men and women.

Caution: Myths Abound

> What are little girls made of?
> Of sugar and spice,

And everything nice,
That's what little girls are made of.

What are little boys made of?
Of snips and snails,
And puppy dog tails,
That's what little boys are made of.

If we trust nursery rhymes for the truth about gender, we might arrive at the conclusion that males and females differ in their very essence. There is no overlap between "sugar and spice and everything nice" and "snips and snails and puppy dog tails." But we do not look to nursery rhymes to answer the question of what it means to be a man or a woman.

Yet even without the nursery rhymes, the moment the subject turns to possible differences between men and women, it is necessary to flag the potholes in the road before us. Gender differences provide fertile ground for the stuff of myths. The first gender myth is a two-headed Hydra.[12] One head is the tendency to exaggerate the differences between men and women. The other head is the denial of any differences between men and women (beyond physiology). Both lead us away from the truth about gender as God's good gift to humanity. When differences are exaggerated, people are often reduced to sets of roles and are denied their full personhood. When differences are denied, God's purposes in creating humanity as male and female may be thwarted.

It is easy to exaggerate differences. For example, some writers draw up lists of characteristics for men and for women. When the categories in such lists are exaggerated to the point of being mutually exclusive, social scientists call this *type-A error* or *alpha-bias*. Type-A error strikes daily in many contexts. For example, on the nightly news a politician exaggerates the difference between the positions of two parties on a bill before Congress. During television commercials, a drug company exaggerates the benefits of its medication over those of competitors in the market. Advertising people constantly look for the real or imagined "edge" they can play up by exaggerating a product's difference from its competitors. Whether the players are politicians, drug manufacturers, or preachers also looking for the "edge" that will make a sermon memorable, a listener must be alert to the exaggeration of differences, simplified to the point of becoming simplistic—and untrue.

Any time a list sets up an extreme comparison, excluding groups of people from one or the other category, type-A error may be present.

For example, a list that states that men are cognitive and women are emotional, or that men are active and women are passive is guilty of alpha-bias. Women as well as men may be cognitive, and men as well as women may be emotional. Women as well as men can be active, and men as well as women can be passive.

On the other hand, because some people simplistically exaggerate differences, others end up denying all differences. This is called *type-B error* or *beta-bias*. Because exaggerated differences are often exploited in hurtful ways,[13] some people choose to discount any legitimate difference that exists. The temptation is strong either to exaggerate differences or to deny them. Both are errors. Both lead to myths that, in the area of gender, do not accurately reflect men's and women's realities.

G. K. Chesterton compared orthodoxy to a narrow ridge between two chasms.[14] The truth about gender difference is also a narrow ridge between the chasm of alpha-bias (exaggerating the difference) and beta-bias (denying the difference). Many books about men and women totter on the brink of or fall into one or the other chasm. In some churches, the difference between men and women may be grossly exaggerated. In fact, it is often stereotyped. On the other hand, many voices in the wider culture call for unisex, declaring that there are no differences between men and women. But the reality is that both are chasms sloping away from the narrow ridge of truth about gender difference.[15]

All of this warns us that it is a complex task to sort out gender issues that impact ministry. We have to monitor ourselves for either alpha-bias or beta-bias. We want to stay on the narrow ridge of the truth about gender and avoid the chasms on either side of us as we explore how gender touches ministry, particularly in the area of preaching.

A second myth—especially when we read popular articles or books about gender difference—lumps all men into one category and all women into the opposite category. It turns out that there is as much diversity *within* a group of women or *within* a group of men as there is *between* men and women. This has been shown to be true in studies of math skills, verbal skills, aggression, and spatial abilities. The *between-group* difference is smaller than the *within-group* difference. One reason for this is that within any general category of difference, other variables factor in. For example, in controlled studies, men in general have better spatial abilities than women. It turns out, however, that gender is not the only factor involved in spatial ability. People who have lived in wide open spaces appear to have better spatial abilities than people who have grown up in confined areas.[16] When it comes to spatial abilities, therefore, gender matters, but environment matters more. And the environment that appears to matter most of all in gender issues is the social environment in which men and women interact.

No behavior, including behavior relating to gender, exists independent of the social context in which it occurs. It is true that if we know the sex of the listener, we know something important. That is good news. As we understand something about the differences and similarities of men and women, we can be more effective preachers. That is the goal of this book. But the bad news is that in considering gender, we can never consider gender per se alone. Gender is rarely, if ever, the only variable we need to take into account if we are to increase the power of God's Word in people's lives.

Ministers who seek to be more effective in sharing God's Word with women face two types of challenge. First, they must understand, at least in part, the experience of women *as women*. Second, they must also understand that the women who listen are not simply generic "women." Each woman is an individual who may be a woman *and* a business executive, or a woman of color, or a single woman living at home and caring for aging parents, or a woman who is divorced and receiving public assistance. She may be a stay-at-home mother with five children. Women are never generic; they are individuals with gender in common but with enormous differences between them. For a preacher, therefore, these differences are as significant as gender in the way each woman will hear the message being preached.

A third myth is that gender is the only factor that matters. Gender matters, but paying attention to gender does not automatically erase the other social factors that, in turn, impact the ways in which women hear a preacher's voice. As a case in point, suppose you are a young, white, unmarried male pastor of an affluent suburban church. A colleague is ill and has asked you to step in and speak to a MOPS[17] group consisting of African American women from an inner-city church in an economically deprived neighborhood. The group includes single mothers receiving public assistance, grandmothers who are primary caregivers of young grandchildren, and young married women working night shifts in order to stay home days with their children. Who is your audience? Women. But is gender the only factor you must consider in answering that question? What is the significance of ethnicity? Of economics? Of marital status? Of age? Of *your* ethnicity? *Your* economics?

Your marital status? *Your* age? Gender matters, but we are closer to the truth in almost every instance if in sharing good news from God, we act on the basis that gender is not the only thing that matters. Many times it may be the least relevant factor to be considered.

When researchers set up a study, they must identify and control all the variables they think might influence the results. For example, if a medical school wants to study the interaction of a particular drug with a specific disease, it is not enough simply to study the drug and the disease in a certain number of infected people. A host of other variables can skew the results of the study unless they are taken into consideration: the patient's age; other medications being used; family history; usual diet, sleep, work, and play habits; addictions; and on and on. Any one of these factors (and others) can mislead researchers if ignored and left out of the study. It is the same when we talk about gender differences. We must nuance carefully what we say about women and men in the pew. There are many variables at work in their lives. Often within-group differences are greater than between-group differences. This should caution us about assuming the myths that may lie behind the assertion that men are from Mars and women are from Venus.

Some Truth about Differences between Men and Women

This leads to the question whether there really are any differences between men and women that *matter* when a preacher steps into the pulpit. To attempt to answer that question, we must distinguish between two interactive parts: our *sex* and our *gender*. They are not synonyms. *Sex* is the biological part of us. It includes all the differences in male and female reproductive structures, the differences in chromosomes (women are XX and men are XY), the differences in hormones (the balance of testosterone and estrogen, for example), and the differences in physical features such as body hair, muscle mass, skin tone, and strength. *Gender,* on the other hand, refers to everything we associate with being *masculine* or *feminine*—the ways we think, feel, and behave that express femininity or masculinity in culturally accepted patterns. As a general rule, therefore, *sex* refers to what is biologically determined and *gender* refers to what is socially learned—the things we have picked up since our infancy about the attitudes and behaviors that are appropriate to being male or female.

Yet there is a strong interaction between our sex and our gender. Look at the role played by essential physiological differences in our reproductive systems. A woman has a uterus and breasts and thus, in most cases, can conceive, give birth to a baby, then nourish that infant. Such abilities have all kinds of ramifications for difference. There is no doubt that women experience physiological events associated with reproduction that have no counterpart in male experience. There is no male corollary to menstruation, pregnancy, parturition, lactation, and the physiology of menopause. Nor do women experience these events only physically. They also experience them emotionally. These events in a woman's body are not just biological. They are integral to the way a woman sees her body and, in many cases, her self-worth and her sexuality.

Does that force us to agree with Sigmund Freud that "biology is destiny"? Not necessarily. Ruth Bleier tells us that "biology defines possibilities but doesn't determine them."[18] Biology is never irrelevant. But neither is it determinant. For each person—male and female—body, mind, behavior, history, and environment interact in unique ways. No two people emerge with exactly the same gender identities.

At issue here is the ongoing debate about gender difference between those who believe that the differences between men and women are innate and those who believe that the differences are the result of life experience. But when we examine a wide range of data, we find that it is not a question of all nature (biology) or all nurture (socialization). There is an interaction between the two in all of us. Some people want to exclude nature entirely and insist on 100 percent nurture. Others want to exclude nurture entirely and insist on 100 percent nature. The truth is somewhere in between. Gender differences do exist. The roots of those differences, however, lie in some combination of nature, nurture, and the environment in which the interaction occurs.

There is a danger in exaggerating the role of nature in the difference. For example, some Christian writers state that God created men to be initiators and women to be responders.[19] If God created men and women thus, then any deviation from that norm in the behavior of a man or a woman is a deviation from God's creational intention. Yet there are Christian men who are uncomfortable in the role of sole initiator, and there are Christian women who do not fit easily into the passive mode of a responder. This is important for you as a preacher to appreciate. If you accept that the differences between men and women are inherent (whether by God's design or biology), you may create great inner conflict and guilt in well-meaning people who do not conform in every way to the model being held up to them as godly or inherent in their being.[20]

You do not preach to a few stereotypes. You speak to individuals in a given social context. To be true to your calling in sharing the Word of God effectively, you must see your listeners as individuals beyond the stereotypes.

Where Do We Go from Here?

In the pages that follow, we want to answer several important questions. What has been learned about contextualized gender differences between men and women? Are these data reliable? If so, what do we do with them? Most important, how do we apply them to preaching?

The chapter title asks, "Is it true that men are from Mars and women are from Venus?" The answer is no. We are all earthlings of the same species, created by a loving God as male and female. There are differences between men and women that come and go, depending on the setting. The challenge is to discern when we are dealing with a myth and when we are dealing with a reality that impacts how we communicate to women.

Summing Up the Chapter

- The closer a preacher's assumptions are to women's realities, the more powerfully will the sermon speak to the issues of women's lives and the needs of their hearts.
- Gender differences provide fertile ground for myths. People who exaggerate the differences between men and women are guilty of type-A error or alpha-bias; people who deny any differences between men and women are guilty of type-B error or beta-bias.
- It is often true that *within*-group differences are greater than *between*-group differences.
- The term *sex* refers to the biological part of us; *gender* refers to the ways we think, feel, and behave that express femininity or masculinity in culturally accepted patterns. Sex is biologically determined; gender is socially learned.

- Biology is never irrelevant, but neither is it determinant.
- Nature and nurture combine in the creation of differences between men and women.
- You do not preach to stereotypes but to individuals.

Questions to Ponder

- As you think about the people to whom you preach, what do you think are their preoccupations through which God's Word must break?
- Think about the last three sermons you preached. What unintended messages might your listeners have heard? Were any of them gender related?
- What do *you* think is the truth about gender differences?
- How does your understanding of gender differences influence your preaching?

2

Preaching for Moral Decision-Making

I had been sitting in the same pew on several consecutive Sundays listening to a series of sermons on the Ten Commandments: You shall have no other gods before me. You shall not make for yourself a carved image. You shall not take the name of the LORD your God in vain. Remember the Sabbath day to keep it holy. Honor your father and your mother. You shall not murder. You shall not commit adultery. You shall not steal. You shall not bear false witness against your neighbor. You shall not covet (Exod. 20:2–17). I had memorized the Ten Commandments as a child, and these "rules of the house" seemed like familiar territory.

But then something new was introduced. The preacher kept pointing us back to the context of the Ten Commandments, to the LORD (Yahweh, the covenant-keeping God-in-relationship), who had brought his people out of the land of bondage and slavery (Exod. 20:2). As I thought about God's care for his people as the context for the commandments, what had seemed to be a list of stern rules began to open up differently. What had looked dry and impersonal came alive when set in the context of God's loving deliverance of his people from slavery. The commandments now appeared to be wise ways of voluntarily staying in relationship with the One who had redeemed me from sin and death. The reasonableness of the Ten

Commandments emerged in new ways when placed in the context of my relationship with God.

The connection should not have surprised me, for Jesus made the link clear for those of us who follow him. One day, a Pharisee who was also a lawyer attempted to trap Jesus with a trick question. He asked, "Teacher, which is the great commandment in the law?" Jesus answered, "'You shall love the LORD your God with all your heart, with all your soul, and with all your mind.' This is the first and great commandment. And the second is like it: 'You shall love your neighbor as yourself.' On these two commandments hang all the Law and the Prophets" (Matt. 22:36–39). Loving God and loving others together summarize not only the Ten Commandments but also all the Law and the Prophets. To keep us from sentimentalizing our relationship with God, however, Jesus reminds us that this love for God flows out of a whole heart, a whole soul, and a whole mind. This chapter and those that follow will explore how that plays out in our daily lives—and in preaching to women.

Loving God with a whole heart sounds somewhat sentimental. But when we probe the verb *love* and the noun *heart,* an unsentimental picture emerges. "To love" in this text has little to do with feelings or emotion; rather, to love *(agapē)* is to seek to do what is in the best interest of the other person (in this case, God). To seek with a whole heart what is best for the other person pushes us out of our twenty-first-century notion of the heart as the seat of our emotions to a first-century view of the heart as the seat of our moral motions, our moral decision-making. Jesus saw the heart as the source of "evil thoughts, murders, adulteries, fornications, thefts, false witness, blasphemies" (Matt. 15:19), cataloguing virtually in order the last half of the Ten Commandments. Elsewhere in Matthew's Gospel, Jesus states that "a good man out of the good treasure of his heart brings forth good things, and an evil man out of the evil treasure brings forth evil things" (12:35). The heart is the seat of volition and the moral life, and loving God with a whole heart includes loving God with our moral will.[1] According to Jesus, our hearts can be the source of all kinds of moral wrong. The antidote to these ethical evils is to love God with a whole heart, not a perverted heart. We make good moral decisions when we make them in the context of our love for God and our neighbor. We show our love for God when we make moral decisions on the basis of what is best for God's reputation in the world.

In light of this discussion, how do *you* feel or think about these "rules of the house," the ethical principles found in Scripture? How do you *preach* the rules of the house?[2] Basic to all religion (Christian and otherwise) are such rules: Some things are to be done and other things are to be avoided. The *way* in which you preach the rules of the house, however, can impact the ways in which your listeners understand and live them out. The house rules govern how people in the house make moral decisions. The manner in which you present them in the pulpit can alter how listeners come to moral decision-making.

On the surface, we might assume that boys and girls growing up in the same church and attending the same confirmation or Sunday school classes will use the same criteria for making moral decisions. After all, they have heard the same teachers and preachers instructing them in the truth of the Bible. We believe that a truth is a truth, and its application should not be too difficult to figure out. Yet some studies on moral development reveal interesting differences between men and women in the moral values they hold and in the ways they apply their moral values to specific life situations.

Moral decision-making (i.e., making decisions about what is right and wrong) is learned over time in the business of living. This process of learning to choose what is right is generally referred to as "moral development." It involves everything from the specific "Thou shalts" of the Ten Commandments to an application of those principles to life issues big and small, personal or abstract: to war and peace, to divorce, to issues such as capital punishment or abortion, or to sex outside marriage. Consider, for example, the situation of a pregnant teenager who is deciding whether to abort or to carry the infant to full term:

- On what criteria or reasons will she make such a decision? What factors will influence her ultimate decision?
- What factors are primary in her parents' decision whether to support their daughter caught in such a bind? As they weigh the situation, what will tip the scale one way or the other in the way they address the issue?
- How will the father of her unborn child consider the decision she makes?
- On what criteria will you as her pastor counsel her about aborting the fetus? What will you give her as reasons to or not to abort?

Each person—the woman herself, her parents, her boyfriend, and her pastor—faces a moral dilemma. Each one will make a moral decision about how to deal with the situation. How will each one reason through this dilemma? What criteria will each one use in weighing the issues? How will each one approach the task of deciding what is right and what is wrong?

Possible Gender Differences in Moral Decision-Making

Current understanding of the ways people learn to make choices about right and wrong has been heavily influenced by studies of moral development conducted by Lawrence Kohlberg. The conclusions Kohlberg reached must be applied carefully, however, because his early studies used only male subjects.[3] He documented changes in the ways eighty-four boys made moral choices over a period of more than twenty years. From his observations, he concluded that people move through six possible stages of moral development.[4] In his later research using this scale, Kohlberg found evidence of gender differences in moral development. For a stage-3 person, for example, doing the right thing means helping and pleasing other people. Stage-4 decisions subordinate relationships to rules. According to Kohlberg, most men eventually reach stage 4 (a law-and-order mentality that measures morality in *im*personal terms), but most women reach only stage 3 (a sense of responsibility to others that measures morality in *inter*personal terms).[5]

Because of this, some people have concluded that women have a less developed sense of morality because, in general, they tend to make a moral decision based on its impact on other people rather than on an impersonal rule or law. In thinking about this alleged "deficiency" in women, we must remember that in his study, Kohlberg developed a scale using males as the norm. He then measured women using the male-based scale and declared women deficient because they differed from his male subjects. The women that Kohlberg studied were no less concerned about moral issues, but their responses were different, and this difference appeared to Kohlberg as a deficiency.

Carol Gilligan, Kohlberg's colleague in some of the moral development studies, notes that the very qualities that define "goodness" in women—their care for and sensitivity to the needs of others—also mark them as deficient in moral judgment when assessed according to Kohlberg's scale.[6] In Kohlberg's judgment, it is inadequate to make a moral decision on the basis of its effect on relationships. People must learn to make moral decisions based on more abstract and impersonal standards.[7] This is a kind of catch-22 for many women. Their sensitivity to the needs of others and the way they assume responsibility for taking care of others often lead women to listen to voices other than their own and to include other points of view when making moral judgments.[8] On Kohlberg's scale, this appears as moral weakness.

Return to the issue about a young woman facing the question of aborting a child. Frederica Mathewes-Green[9] spent a year interviewing post-abortion women in various parts of North America. She found that in many cases young women decided to abort because either their parents or the father of the unborn child insisted that they abort. Parents were often most concerned about the opinions of their own peers and did not want to experience the shame associated with having their daughter give birth to a child out of wedlock. Or they felt that an untimely pregnancy would destroy their daughter's potential education or career. The boys or men who fathered these babies were, for the most part, not interested in the consequences of their actions and did not want the inconvenience of parenthood (or child support) at that point in their lives. The women chose to abort because they wanted to retain the goodwill of the people most significant to them.[10]

For most Christians, the fact that some women choose to abort a child on the basis of important ongoing relationships with their parents or a boyfriend is an inadequate reason to do so. They would hold that the larger principle of the sacredness of human life must prevail. This would support Kohlberg's understanding of mature moral development: We must move beyond an interpersonal basis for decision-making to the use of rules or abstract principles.

Because Kohlberg has made moral development a primary focus of his research, he has examined the question of moral decision-making from many angles. In one research project, a moral dilemma was posed to a group of eleven-year-old children (in this case, both boys and girls),[11] asking how it should be resolved. The dilemma was this: A man named Heinz considers whether he should steal a medication that he cannot afford to buy in order to save the life of his wife. He has asked the pharmacist to reduce the price, but the pharmacist has refused to do so. What should Heinz do? This is a conflict between moral norms. The researchers were interested in the logic used by young adolescents in resolving it.

According to Gilligan, eleven-year-old Jake was clear from the outset that Heinz should steal the medication. He reasoned that the conflict was between the values of property and human life and that life is more valuable than property.[12] Jake called this dilemma "sort of like a math problem with humans" and worked out the solution that Heinz should steal the medication. He concluded that if Heinz were caught and put on trial, the judge would see the morality of his action and would not punish him for his theft.

Gilligan also reports the response of Amy, who came at the problem in a completely different way. Amy said, "I think there might be other ways besides stealing it," reasoning that perhaps Heinz could get a loan. While she was certain that Heinz should not steal the medication, she was also certain that his wife should not be allowed to die. If Heinz stole the medicine, he might save his wife's life for the moment. But if he had to go to jail for the theft, his wife might get sick again, and he would not be there to care for her. At risk were the ongoing relationships both between Heinz and his wife and between Heinz and the druggist. There had to be another way to solve the problem.

Amy saw the dilemma not as "a math problem with humans" (as Jake did) but as an unfolding story of relationships extending over time. She was concerned about the wife's continuing need for her husband and for the pharmacist's need to respond to the family situation. In Gilligan's analysis, Amy was looking at a world made up of relationships rather than of people standing alone, a world held together through human connection rather than through a system of rules. For Amy, the problem was the pharmacist's failure to respond to human need. She assumed that if the pharmacist could see the consequences of his refusal to lower his price, he would give the medicine to Heinz for his wife and let him pay later.

These two young adolescents saw the same dilemma as two very different moral problems. To Jake, it was a conflict between the value of life and the value of property, and it could be resolved by logical deduction: Life has a higher value than property, so in this case stealing would be appropriate.[13] To Amy, the problem was a fracture in human relationships. Jake saw the problem through systems of logic and law. For Amy, the solution lay in developing a process of communication in relationship.[14]

When their responses were evaluated by the interviewer in the research project, however, Amy scored a full stage lower than Jake because she did not demonstrate an ability to think systematically about the concepts of morality or law. The interviewer considered her reliance on relationships naive and immature. In the end, the interviewer measured what Jake saw that Amy failed to see but never asked what Amy saw that Jake failed to see. Amy's responses fell through the sieve of Kohlberg's scoring system, and she was considered deficient in moral judgment.[15]

As Gilligan worked alongside Kohlberg at Harvard on issues of moral judgment, she became convinced that, in general, the male approach to ethical decision-making focuses on the morality of rights based on equality and is centered on an understanding of fairness.[16] In essence, moral decisions must be made by applying the principle of fairness equally to all people, and we do this through impersonal rules. In contrast, the female approach to moral development focuses on an ethic of responsibility that recognizes differences in need. People's life situations are unique because the individuals participating in any interaction are unique. Thus, a one-size-fits-all approach to making moral decisions is inadequate. It is essential to take the uniqueness of each situation into consideration.

Do you remember being shown in school a picture of a woman: Looked at one way, the woman is young and beautiful; looked at another way, she is an old hag. Or perhaps you were shown a figure of two squiggly vertical lines and were asked what you saw. To some in the class, the two lines together formed a vase; to others, they formed the profiles of two women looking at each other. When your teacher showed you these pictures, you were probably studying the ways in which people see and interpret reality. It is interesting that even after you were told how to see both pictures in the picture, something inside you pushed you to see one over the other.[17]

The same kind of thing happens when men and women develop moral judgment. Some may choose to view morality primarily in terms of justice or fairness; others may choose to view morality in terms of care. That choice (between justice and care) changes the way we define a moral problem. The problem is different because the "picture" is different. We see that in the hypothetical situation Jake and Amy faced: Jake formed his solution on the basis of justice, and Amy formed hers on the basis of care. For him, stealing the drug was legitimate because the druggist was unfair or unjust in the face of Heinz's dilemma. For her, nothing legitimated the risk of stealing the drug because Heinz's wife needed the ongoing care her husband could give her.

Gilligan[18] concluded that "girls . . . develop a basis for 'empathy' built into their primary definition of self in a way that boys do not. . . . Girls emerge with a stronger basis for experiencing another's needs or feelings as one's own."[19] Consequently, relationships are experienced differently by women and men.[20] In fact, if Gilligan is correct, the very concept of *relationship* may carry different meanings and significance for men and women, beginning in early childhood.

It is possible to make too much of Gilligan's observations. Her conclusions are based on small samples. Is there any corroborating evidence from other researchers of gender differences between girls and boys and men and women in moral development?

Researcher Janet Lever spent considerable time observing fifth-grade boys and girls during recess on a school playground. She noted that boys played in larger and age-heterogeneous groups, while girls tended toward activities within groups of two or three. Boys usually played much more competitive games than did girls. Girls were more likely to play turn-taking games such as hopscotch or jump rope rather than games in which there is a winner and a loser.

She also noted that boys' games generally lasted longer than girls' games because boys settled disputes by elaborating on the rules, enabling them to keep playing the game. Lever observed that boys quarreled all the time, but although a game could be interrupted because of a quarrel, no game was delayed for more than seven minutes. Boys seemed to enjoy the legal debates involved in elaborating on the rules of the game as much as they enjoyed the game itself. Girls, on the other hand, tended to end the game whenever disputes broke out. Preserving relationships appeared to be more important than continuing the game.[21]

The Swiss psychologist Jean Piaget found that boys become increasingly fascinated throughout childhood with the legal elaboration of rules and the development of fair procedures for settling conflicts. In his studies, this fascination did not characterize girls. Piaget wrote that girls have a more pragmatic attitude toward rules, "regarding a rule as good as long as the game repaid it."[22] He noted that girls are more tolerant in their attitudes toward rules, more willing to make exceptions, and more easily reconciled to innovations. As a result, *the legal sense*, which Piaget considered essential to moral development, "is far less developed in little girls than in boys."[23]

Jean Baker Miller states that "women stay with, build on, and develop in a context of attachment and affiliation with others. . . . Women's sense of self becomes very much organized around being able to make, and then to maintain, affiliations and relationships." When a relationship is disrupted, many women see this not just as "a loss of the relationship, but as something closer to a loss of her own self."[24]

In 1929, Virginia Woolf wrote, "It is obvious that the values of women differ very often from the values which have been made by the other sex. . . . It is the masculine values that prevail."[25] Therein lies a problem that can be particularly acute for Christian women. In much preaching, the "masculine value" of rules and principles prevails over relationships. Yet if Miller is correct that women's sense of self is organized around their ability to make and maintain relationships, that affiliation cannot help but impact moral decision-making. As a consequence, women (and Christian women in particular) may come to question whether they can legitimately include concern for others when making moral decisions. (This is strange inasmuch as Scripture puts a strong emphasis on love in our relationships with our neighbors.) But because relationships are so integral to most women's sense of personhood, women often do defer to the opinions of others and alter their judgments accordingly. We see this in the way many women express what they believe to be true. Like Tevye in *Fiddler on the Roof*, they speak with divided judgments, qualifying statements with "On the one hand . . . On the other hand . . ."

To some observers, this apparent confusion of judgment looks like moral weakness, but Gilligan and others see it as inseparable from women's moral strength—a deep concern for relationships. It is possible that many women's reluctance to judge may itself be a mark of their concern for others that is intrinsic to their development. Two things happen simultaneously: Women tend to define themselves in terms of relationships, and they also evaluate themselves morally in terms of their ability to care.

Yet as Woolf noted, it is the masculine values that prevail. Thus, Christian women often find themselves on the horns of a dilemma: Should they make moral decisions on the basis of rules and abstract principles (ignoring their concern for others), or should they make moral decisions on the basis of what seems best for all parties concerned, regardless of the rules or abstract principles?

Thus, the gender issues involved in moral reasoning reflect different questions: Do we see moral problems arising from a conflict in our responsibilities to others, or do we see them arising from competing rights enunciated in abstract principles, laws, or rules?[26] For many women, what appears to be a male morality of rights seems to justify indifference to human need and unconcern for individuals. On the other hand, for most men, a female morality based on responsibility to others seems inconclusive and diffuse because the decision may be different depending on the context. There is nothing crisp or definite about this morality. There is no rule that always applies equally in every case.

Apart from academic studies of moral development, much of Madison Avenue operates on the perception that most women are embedded in relationships. Why are television "soaps" broadcast in the afternoon? Because women, more of whom are home in the afternoon compared to men, are the major consumers of these ongoing (never-ending) stories of overly entwined relationships. Why are romance novels the bread and butter of certain publishing firms? Because enough women crave these narratives of love and loss and suffering, built on interwoven relationships, to keep romance novels near or at the top of all book sales in North America. Women, in general, appear to be much more oriented to interdependence than to what they see as masculine individualism.

Many (not all) women experience conflict over competition. We see this not only in Lever's studies of children at play but also in many women's antipathy toward professional sports. This is particularly true of violent sports (such as hockey or football), but it is true in some measure of any competitive team sport in which there must be losers as well as winners. Women in general appear to be more committed to seeking win-win situations, looking for ways to resolve dilemmas by means that do not threaten relationships.

A further observation emerging from these studies is that most women are quick to subordinate their own achievement to caring for someone else, and they place a higher value on connectedness than on personal achievement.[27] At the same time, studies of women in the workplace have shown that women who have been trained by men on the job often bring a more competitive attitude to their work.[28] When women labor in a male-dominated work environment, they often set aside altruistic behaviors in favor of an aggressiveness that matches that of their male coworkers. This should serve as a caution against inferring that women are inherently more altruistic than men. The social context influences their ethic of caring. Both women and men have shown their willingness to abandon both caring and justice in social settings that encouraged competitiveness.

It is relevant to the preaching task that at least half the women in your church spend time (eight or more hours a day) in the working world, where "caring" is difficult at best and often impossible. The shift in moral decision-making required for women to be successful in the business world is unrecognized (and largely unstudied) and is also a major factor in the stress that working women experience. At the same time, some studies of women CEOs have emphasized a different approach to the world of work that more closely parallels gender differences in moral development.[29] (This is discussed at greater length in chapter 8.)

As stated in the previous chapter, differences *within* groups may be as important as differences *between* groups. Not all women make moral decisions based on relationships, nor do all men make moral decisions based on rules, laws, or internalized principles.[30] In real life, according to Carol Tavris, "no individual is strictly autonomous or connected."[31] We find warrant for seeking both connection and autonomy because each is a necessary condition of the other.[32]

How Does This Apply to Preaching?

Reports of Gilligan's investigation of women's moral reasoning were first published in her book titled *In a Different Voice*. With a description of women's different reasoning, the issue on the table became clear. For a decision to be maximally moral, must it be based on law-and-order criteria, or is the "different voice" of relationship an equally valid criterion for choosing one path over another? In the field of Christian ethics (and most sermons reflect ethical thought), a majority of evangelical moral theologians have labeled themselves "deontologists," that is, those who are concerned with our obligations under law. But others have followed a different path, one that H. Richard Niebuhr called "the responsible self."[33] He maintained that it is in our interaction with those around us that our moral response is shaped as one of responsibility to others.[34]

Early in this chapter the question was asked, How do you preach the "rules of the house"? The prior question may well be, What do your people need to hear from the pulpit in order to love God with all their hearts? The Great Commandment is for both men and women: How do you preach God's truth so that the whole church can hear and obey? When you address issues of moral decision-making, you may approach the biblical text only through a lens of logic and law, or you may set up the issue in terms of relationships—how others will be affected and what can be done to preserve or develop the relationships involved in the dilemma. As you prepare to preach on a particular text, you must judge whether impersonal rules take precedence over interpersonal relationships or vice versa, or if there is a way to address the moral issues of a text that takes both sides into account. Some men and women in the pews will "hear" the impersonal well; others may be listening for the interpersonal in order to interpret what is being said.

Men and women who take the Scriptures seriously have to ask whether Kohlberg's schema corresponds to the teaching of the Bible. Kohlberg sets the impersonal rule level of moral development higher than the interpersonal relationship level. But is that a biblical way of thinking? A useful starting point in responding to that question is Matthew 5, in which Jesus reinterprets some of the Ten Commandments for his listeners. The context of his review of those commandments is his statement in verse 20: "I say to you, that unless your righteousness exceeds the righteousness of the scribes and Pharisees, you will by no means enter the kingdom of heaven." Immediately following that statement he begins the review of several of the commandments, starting each with these words: "You have heard that it was said to those of old . . ." (vv. 21, 27, 31, 33). After the statement of the Old Testament commandment, he goes on to say, "But I say to you that . . ." (vv. 22, 28, 32, 34).

The structure of Matthew 5 makes it clear that Jesus is teaching us how we are to think about, interpret, and use the Ten Commandments, the rules of the house. In other words, he is instructing us in moral decision-making by taking us back to the great principles laid out by God to the people of God in Exodus 20 and Deuteronomy 5.

Who among Jesus' audiences in the first century kept those commandments most scrupulously? The Pharisees, of course. Yet Jesus opened this part of the Sermon on the Mount by stating clearly that "unless your righteousness *exceeds* the righteousness of the scribes and Pharisees, you will by no means enter the kingdom of heaven" (v. 20).

How could the ordinary villagers thronging to hear him do better than the Pharisees? It seemed impossible. The answer to the question lies, however, in the way in which people in Jesus' time heard and understood the word *righteousness*. Elizabeth Achtemeier explains:

> Righteousness as it is understood in the Old Testament is a thoroughly Hebraic concept, foreign to the Western mind and at variance with the common understanding of the term. The failure to comprehend its meaning is perhaps most responsible for the view of the Old Testament religion as "legalistic" and as far removed from the graciousness of the New Testament.[35]

She goes on to state that righteousness is *always* the fulfillment of the demands of a relationship—whether between us and God or among ourselves. Righteousness is "right-relatedness."

When Jesus spoke of righteousness in Matthew 5:20, he had in mind the Old Testament sense of righteousness as right-relatedness. We are rightly related to God through the sacrifice of Christ, and we are rightly related to one another as we live by God's practical commands for daily life.

- If we are righteous or rightly related to one another, we will see that it is not enough to refrain from murder (5:21); we must guard against anger without a cause and anger that leads to angry words (v. 22). We are always to seek reconciliation (v. 23–24), the mending of relationship.
- If we are righteous or rightly related to one another, we will go beyond the technicalities of not committing adultery (v. 27) and will deal mercilessly and permanently with the beginnings of lust in our own minds and hearts (vv. 28–30). If we are rightly related to one another, we will not look for a loophole allowing us to divorce a spouse (v. 32), thus destroying a relationship.

To see this worked out, we need look only at our Lord in his earthly ministry. Jesus continually confounded his critics by his insistence on cultivating right relationships. In Luke 7, we see the Pharisees muttering about the woman of the streets anointing Jesus' feet with perfume, while Jesus shows his care for her. In Luke 19, we see Jesus choosing to go home with an outcast tax collector named Zacchaeus, while bystanders question his choice of friends. In John 4, we see Jesus initiating a conversation with a woman who had more than one strike against her. Even his disciples are puzzled that he is bothering to talk with her. Again and again, he is concerned about relationships, not about legalisms.

At the root of righteous (moral) living lies right-relatedness. Can you see the implications of this for preaching? How would *you* preach on the Ten Commandments? Would you preach them merely as rules for life or as universal principles and apply them in a one-size-fits-all manner? Or would you preach them as grounded first in our relationship with God and then in our specific relationships with our families and communities?

At the same time, this is not an either-or issue. Ethical decision-making in the Bible demands that dual attention be given to the principles *and* to the context in which they are applied. The prophet Micah asked, "What does the LORD require of you?" The answer was, "To act justly *and* to love mercy *and* to walk humbly with your God" (Micah 6:8 NIV, emphasis added). The coordinating conjunctions *(and)* in that sentence make it clear that the question is not one of "acting justly" *or* "loving mercy." We should do both. This brings what is considered to be a masculine focus on abstract principles and a feminine focus on the human context of their application into play. It is not enough to preach the principles without mercy or concern for those affected by those principles. Nor can we sacrifice the principles to individual situations. We are called to preach God's truth through the use of both principles and contexts. The interaction between the two is like a dance.

Ruth Tiffany Barnhouse offers a helpful analogy by pointing us to the human eye. As a physician, she describes the functions of the two kinds of vision that make up our sightedness.[36] We have macular vision, which allows us to focus on detail, and we have peripheral vision, which gives us the context of a particular detail. Were we to ask, "Which is most important—macular or peripheral vision?" the sane response, of course, would be, "That's a nonsense question—we need both." Without macular vision, whatever we viewed would be fuzzy, but without peripheral vision, we might not understand what we were scrutinizing because we would not have the context that explained it. Context without focus is inadequate. Focus without context is inadequate. We must have both—in preaching as well as in sightedness.

We need to focus on universal principles, but we understand them best (perhaps only) in the concrete contexts in which they are applied. When Jesus applied God's commandments to people in first-century Israel, he did not allow the commandments to stand without a strong personal application to real impediments in relationships with others. Without the necessary relational piece, our "righteousness" is no better than that of the Pharisees to whom the doors of heaven were shut (Matt. 5:20; 23:13).

Loving God with whole hearts means making moral decisions that combine both justice and mercy, both law and context. When you preach the whole counsel of God, men and women will make righteous, moral decisions—decisions rooted in their concern for right-relatedness with God and their neighbor.

Summing Up the Chapter

- Because our hearts can be the source of all kinds of moral wrong, the antidote to these ethical evils is to love God with a whole heart.
- The *way* you preach the rules of the house can alter the basis on which your listeners make moral decisions.
- In much preaching, the "masculine value" of rules or principles prevails over relationships.
- The gender issues involved in moral reasoning reflect different questions: Do we see moral problems arising from a conflict in our responsibilities to others, or do we see them arising from competing rights?
- The question every preacher must wrestle with biblically and theologically is how to preach on moral issues.
- At the root of righteous (moral) living lies right-relatedness.
- Ethical decision-making in the Bible demands that dual attention be given to the principles *and* to the context in which they are applied.

Questions to Ponder

- What kind of "righteousness" is to characterize those of us who carry the name of Christ into the world?
- What is a biblical understanding of moral development and moral decision-making?
- How do we apply that biblical understanding in our own lives? In our preaching?
- How does our biblical understanding of moral decision-making influence how we minister to men and women in the church? To men and women outside the church?
- As you think back over the last three sermons you preached, how well did you balance abstract principles with the relational context in which they are to be applied?
- Fundamentally, do you see the rules of the house as one size fits all, or is there room for different applications in different contexts?
- How did Jesus sum up the "rules" of the law?

3

Preaching for Psychological Wholeness

Several years ago while on vacation, my husband and I visited a nearby church one Sunday. During the congregational announcements, the pastor called three women to the pulpit: "Come on up here, girls, so everyone can see your pretty faces. Tell everybody about the bake sale coming up." At that point three older, white-haired women rose from their pews and moved toward the platform. "Girls"? "Pretty faces"? My husband and I looked at each other with amazement. The women were hardly girls. Whether or not they had pretty faces was not particularly relevant to the announcement they were called to make. I am sure that to the jocular pastor that day, the comment was harmless, even complimentary in some general way. Yet behind the comment lay assumptions about women and what matters to them (being girls and being pretty). Later in his sermon (the text of which I have forgotten), the pastor preached to gender stereotypes. That is, he pigeonholed men and women in ways that did not allow them to have their full personhood before God.

What does it mean to be a man or a woman created in the image of God? Is it relevant to define gender in ways that deny men their full range of emotions or that deny women the full use of their minds or gifts? This chapter goes behind the stereotypes that sometimes creep into churches and sermons and then looks at how these stereotypes affect men and women in the pews.

The central task of preaching is to enable listeners to love the LORD (Yahweh, the covenant-keeping God-in-relationship) with all their hearts, with all their souls, with all their minds, and with all their strength, and their neighbor as themselves (Lev. 19:18; Deut. 6:5). This, according to Jesus, sums up all the law and the prophets (Matt. 22:37–40; Luke 10:27–28).[1] The one who helps listeners know God as the LORD will not neglect evangelism but will work to bring people into a love relationship with the LORD God through Jesus Christ. Such a preacher will not neglect worship but will help listeners experience love for God with all their hearts, souls, minds, and strength. Such a preacher will not neglect social concern but will enable listeners to understand how to love a neighbor. But we must ask ourselves, what does it *mean* to love God with all our hearts, all our souls, all our minds, and all our strength? What does it *mean* to love a neighbor as intensely as we love and nurture ourselves?

It is not accidental that when the Ten Commandments are repeated in Deuteronomy 5:6–21, they are almost immediately followed by the Great Commandment, to love God with all our hearts, all our souls, and all our strength (Deut. 6:5). It is easy to replace our love for the LORD with obedience to a formal code of law, missing the essential connection between the two. This distorts God's intention for his people. The law is necessary because God's will is not yet fully grounded in our hearts.[2] But it is a law lived in the context of love for God, who first loved us (1 John 4:19). Chapter 2 examined the danger of failing to preach the "rules of the house" in the context of love for God and our neighbor. Loving God with a whole heart, according to some commentators, includes loving God with our will, the seat of volition and the moral life.

But we are also to love God with all our souls. While we moderns tend to use the word *soul* in the philosophical Greek sense of an immortal entity, the Hebrew Old Testament refers to the soul as the vital life principle in contrast to inert dust. It carries a psychophysical sense of the self animating a body.[3] The Hebrew word *nephesh,* translated as "soul" in most English translations of the Old Testament, often means "self" or "person." In Exodus 23:9, it means "totality of human feeling."[4] The translation of the Old Testament into Greek (the Septuagint) used *psychē* to express the meaning of "soul." It is the word used by Mark as he described Jesus' wrestling in Gethsemane before his arrest and crucifixion: "My soul is exceedingly sorrowful, even to death" (Mark 14:34). John used the same word as he reported Jesus' reflections when told that certain Greeks wanted to see him: "The hour has come that the

Son of Man should be glorified. . . . Now My soul is troubled, and what shall I say? 'Father, save Me from this hour'? But for this purpose I came to this hour" (John 12:23, 27). The apostle Paul used this same Greek word to express the "natural" person in contrast to the "spiritual" person (1 Cor. 2:14). In general, in the New Testament, *psychē* continues the old Greek usage (characteristic, for example, of Homer) by which it means "vitality, life."[5]

> In Jn 19:30 we read: "Jesus gave up his *pneuma* to the Father," and in the same gospel (Jn 10:15), Jesus gave up His "*psuchē [psychē]* for the sheep," and in Mt 20:28, He gave His *psuchē* (not his *pneuma*) as a ransom—a difference which is characteristic: for the *pneuma* stands in quite different relation to God from the *psuchē*. The "spirit" *(pneuma)* is the outbreathing of God into the creature, the life-principle derived from God. The "soul" *(psuchē)* is man's individual possession, that which distinguishes one man from another and from inanimate nature. . . . "Man is not a spirit, but *has* it; he is *soul*. . . . In the soul . . . lies the individuality—in the case of man, his personality, his self, his ego" [quotation is from Oehler, *OT Theology*, I, 217].[6]

While biblical writers sometimes used *heart* and *soul* in overlapping ways, in general, loving God with all our souls implies loving God with the vital psychological part of our being.

We know that the Great Commandment states that we are to love the LORD our God with *all* our souls.[7] Yet both our observations of others and our experiences within ourselves tell us that loving God with all our souls depends in some way on having "whole" souls, souls that are not divided or fractured by our perceptions of life experiences. The proliferation of counseling services in our culture[8] points to the need of many people for help in healing the psychological wounds and splits that keep them from being able to love God or others with their whole psychological beings. The fact is that most of us do not love God with our whole souls because in one way or another we are not psychologically "whole."

How can you preach so that those who listen, especially women, will be able to love God with their whole or entire souls? How can the preached Word free people to love God wholly? What are some of the barriers, particularly for women, that may keep them from loving God with all their souls? One way we know that something is amiss for many women (including Christian women) in our culture is that women continue to be the primary consumers of counseling services in North America. Why do you think this might be so? What could this tell you about women's general happiness and contentedness? What might this say about the adequacy of the Christian message that women hear in church?[9]

Psychological Differences between Men and Women

Reports of differences between men and women reveal at least three areas of difference that may help us understand why more women than men use counseling services:

1. Men and women may not handle stress in the same ways.
2. They may not feel the same about their competencies.
3. They may experience depression for different reasons and handle it in different ways.

Look at each of these through a lens of psychological wholeness.

Stress

People manage stress in daily life differently. One study[10] found that no matter what the cause of stress, people tend to cope with it in one of three ways:

1. Some individuals modify the situation that causes the stress: They make changes in their environment.
2. Others change the meaning or value they place on the stressful situation.
3. Still others manage their emotions about the situation, often denying what they feel.

The first of these three ways of coping with stress focuses on the situation itself. The second and third focus on feelings or beliefs about the situation.

This study also reported interesting differences between men and women. Faced with a stressful situation, men most often choose the first option: They deal straightforwardly with the situation causing the stress. In short, men tend to reduce their stress by changing the circumstances causing the stress. On the other hand, women most often choose the third option: They tend to manage their emotions about the stress rather than changing the stressful circumstances.

Social scientists give various reasons for this difference between men's and women's behaviors. Some social scientists believe men possess "instrumental" traits in contrast to women, who possess "expressive" traits. In a case such as stress management, that means men are more "instrumental" in doing things, changing situations, whereas women, feeling powerless, doubt their ability to change situations and thus deal with their emotions about things that cause stress.[11] The moment anyone (male or female) allows stress to get inside his or her emotions, managing that stress becomes a more difficult problem. This usually involves self-talk, telling ourselves that we shouldn't worry. The researchers found that people using the third way of coping with stress use denial, passive acceptance, withdrawal, an element of magical thinking, a hopefulness bordering on blind faith, and belief that the avoidance of worry and tension is the same as problem-solving.[12] This helps us understand why women report higher levels of stress than do men: Many women choose the least effective method to handle a stressful situation.[13] Attempting to manage one's emotions about stressful events or relationships seldom reduces stress for the long term.

Why would many women choose this least effective method? The answer has disturbing and sad implications for the preaching task: Many women do not understand that they have other options. They have been taught that being passive is a proper female posture in life. Generally, women do not believe that they have the power, authority, or competency to act to change the stressful situations in which they find themselves. Only men have that power or authority.

Women's general disbelief in their ability to change their circumstances ought to be of deep concern to pastors. A fundamental aim of preaching is to empower listeners to incorporate what they have heard from Scripture into solutions to the challenges of everyday life. Yet if women do not believe that as *women* they can act, they will not hear your message of empowerment in the same way that men might hear it. When women hear a sermon on Philippians 4:13 ("I can do all things through Christ who strengthens me," the context of which is how to deal with anxiety about a host of problems, including the meeting of basic needs), they may not hear the empowerment in that text.

Self-esteem

In 1991, *Christianity Today* carried an unsettling editorial written by David Neff:

> The dense smoke rising from the women's ordination debate may be clouding our view of an important factor—one that should concern us no matter what our position on ordination: there is a woeful lack of self-respect among an entire category of Christian women.
>
> Gary Bredfeldt, chair of the Ontario Bible College department of ministry studies, recently demonstrated that entering women students at nine Canadian Bible colleges were seriously lacking in measures of self-esteem,[14] self-confidence, and a sense of personal competence. In the general population, women of the same age rank about 7% behind men on a standard measure of feelings of personal competence. In the Bible college sample, the gap was an appalling 40%. The Bible college women rated 20% lower than women at secular institutions, while the Bible college men rated 15% above their secular counterparts. Although Bredfeldt's study gives only preliminary results, it ought not to be ignored.
>
> Students of women's psychology have long noted the confidence gap between men and women. . . . Rosalind Barnett and Grace Baruch noted in *The Competent Woman*, "When failure occurs, women are the ones who tend to believe [that] their *abilities* are inadequate, men to believe that their *efforts* [are] insufficient. When success occurs, on the other hand, women tend to think that the task must have been easy, or that luck was with them; men credit their own abilities." Granted that this confidence gap exists, we must wonder why it is exacerbated in some Christian circles.[15]

The issue raised in Neff's editorial cannot be ignored. Although care must be taken in applying the results of this study to the broader Christian community, it nevertheless raises some serious questions about Christian women and their self-esteem. Why is the disparity (40 percent) between the Christian men's and women's self-esteem so much greater than the much smaller difference (7 percent) among their peers in the general Canadian population? What factors in their upbringing or in their present situation (students enrolled in Bible colleges) might explain the self-esteem of these young Christian women in comparison to the ratings of their peers in secular colleges or universities? And what are we to make of the fact that at the same time, the self-esteem of Christian young men appears to be significantly higher than that of their male peers? Bredfeldt's report points to the disturbing possibility that some of the Christian women listening to your sermons may also suffer from a profound disbelief in their worth and abilities.

Of course, a sample of Bible college women in nine Canadian schools probably does not reflect the self-esteem of all or most women sitting in the pews in your church. But other researchers suggest that self-esteem issues for women are more pervasive than we might want to believe. Peggy Orenstein[16] documents that while girls in the first grade begin with the same level of skills and ambition as the boys, by the time they reach high school, their doubts have crowded out their dreams. Mary Pipher[17] reports that as girls reach junior high school, their math scores plummet and depression levels rise as their self-esteem crumbles. She identifies emphases and trends in the wider culture that make it difficult for a girl to develop psychological wholeness in today's Western world. At the same time, recent studies of adolescent boys[18] have turned up evidence of a disturbing drop in boys' self-esteem, reversing earlier trends. This generation's boys are sad, lonely, and confused, even though they may appear to be tough, cheerful, and confident. Low self-esteem, therefore, is becoming an important concern for young men as well as for young women. Christians surely must be concerned to find ways to understand how our culture undermines the confidence, expectations, and optimism of both boys and girls.

Generally speaking, self-esteem is a product of the value we assign ourselves as we believe ourselves to be (i.e., our self-worth) blended with the value we assign to our abilities.[19] For Christian men and women alike, a biblically valid sense of self-esteem must incorporate the acknowledgment that we are sinners and, consequently, that we are objects of God's continuous grace. None of us can live above that dependence on God's mercy and kindness toward us in every aspect of life. But at the same time, biblical self-esteem also affirms the individual as a person of worth whom God has called and gifted. We are designed to serve God fully with the gifts he has given us. Yet some people hear the message of condemnation (sinful human depravity) and miss the message of worth before God. Many women have great difficulty affirming joyfully their creation in the *imago Dei* and the gifts and calling of God in their lives. Self-esteem (whether it is low or high) shapes the way the message is heard, and women often do not hear the biblical message of empowerment in the same way men do.

Developing and maintaining a biblically valid sense of self-esteem is a complex task for both men and women. As one of the gifts of God's boundless grace, Scripture gives Christians the necessary spiritual and psychological resources to do this successfully.[20] It is part of the preacher's task, however, to explain how men and women can use these resources to respond to life in a positive, biblically responsible way. To be effective, however, the minister must not only communicate a biblically sound theology but also put the message into the differing life experiences of men and women in the pews. For example, when you preach about pride, men are more likely to objectify it as striving for position in the marketplace or the church. Women, however, may confuse what you are saying with legitimate self-esteem. It is the same message, but if it is not applied specifically, it may lead to very different results.

Depression

A third element that affects women's life experiences is the complex condition generally identified as depression.[21]

> A person with major depression has frequent episodes of hopelessness and low self-esteem, with an absence of pleasure in nearly all activities. So many people experience depression that it is often called the "common cold" of psychological disorders. . . . Unfortunately, women are 1.7 to 3.0 times more likely than men to experience depression during their lifetime.[22]

Some clinicians estimate informally than as many as 85 percent of their clients are depressed women. A 3-to-1 ratio of depression in women compared to men raises a question: Are women more vulnerable to depression than are men? Some clinicians would argue that depression is underdiagnosed in men because men are less likely than women to seek help for depression.[23] Other clinicians report that for every man diagnosed with depression, at least two and up to six women are diagnosed as clinically depressed.[24]

Margaret Matlin has identified seven personal and social factors that relate to depression:

1. little sense of control over one's life
2. low self-esteem
3. low sense of personal accomplishment
4. derived identity, a strong sense that one's personal identity depends on another person's accomplishments
5. little social support from friends and family

6. worry about relationships with significant others
7. traditional, feminine gender-typing[25]

While some of these are common to both men and women, others are more specific to women. In general, women appear to be more vulnerable to all of them.

Depression resembles grief because in both, feelings of loss and sadness dominate the emotions.[26] Depression, however, is not identical to grief. Individuals suffering from depression also experience a drop in self-esteem. In addition, depressed people show additional symptoms that affect thinking, sleep, appetite, energy level, and behavior. Although these symptoms are common to both depressed men and depressed women, some observers suggest that within the common experience of grief and loss, men and women are responding to different kinds of losses. Women most often report being depressed because of a disruption or conflict in a close relationship. Men often report being depressed because of the loss of an ideal or an achievement-related goal or because of performance issues.[27]

Two different ideas of the self may underlie these differing experiences of depression in women and men. One picture of the inner self has been labeled the *separate self.*[28] This picture reflects the prototypical American vision of the rugged individual, the hero, the warrior, the self-made man. A person with this kind of picture of the inner self focuses on control, self-direction, and independence. For a person characterized by the separate self, relationships are *functional.* This person acknowledges the reality of personal needs that others can meet and enters into relationships primarily to have those needs met. This process, of course, is usually not carried out in an obvious or crude manner, devoid of attachments. But for this type of person, relationships are not valuable in and of themselves. Relationships primarily serve the purposes of the separate self even as that person reciprocally serves some needs in another person. B. Ehrenreich and D. English described the consequences of this approach to relationships:

> If [my needs] are no longer being satisfied by a friend or sexual partner, then that bond may be broken just as reasonably as a buyer would take his business away from a seller if he found a better price. The *needs* have an inherent legitimacy—the *people* are replaceable.[29]

Similarly, Dana Crowley Jack observed:

> If relationships are functional in this economic sense, then the deterioration or loss of a particular relationship should not strike the individual to the core, and the goal should be to replace the lost relationship with as little disruption as possible.[30]

Some have suggested that the picture of the inner self as the separate self is characteristic of many men. At the conclusion of *Men and Masculinity,* Roy McCloughry comments with a certain sadness that "conventional masculinity is very functional. It is about getting things done, being in control, solving problems and not being vulnerable."[31]

A second possible picture of the inner self has been labeled the *relational self.* In contrast to the separate self, this self is defined in the context of a social experience: I understand who I am (as a self) as I see your reaction to me—to my words and my actions.[32] For the individual with this personal picture of the inner self, a relationship is *not* merely functional; it provides a foundation or basis for personal identity. For those with an inner vision of the relational self, attachments are the soil in which the self grows.

Nancy Chodorow found that significant differences generally mark the early childhood experiences of boys and girls.[33] Girls experience themselves as "less separate" than boys. In other words, they develop a picture of the inner self that is relational. This leads to a different way of experiencing loss. It also leads to a different response to depression or a sense of loss.

> Susan Nolen-Hoeksema found that when men are depressed, they are likely to distract themselves from their emotions through some sort of activity, an approach she calls a *distracting style* of responding to depression. In contrast, when women are depressed, they are likely to focus inward on their symptoms by contemplating the possible causes and consequences of their emotions, an approach she calls a *ruminative style* of response. . . . People who engage in distraction are often successful in lifting themselves out of depression. . . . In contrast, rumination prolongs and intensifies a bad move. Rumination tends to create a negative bias in people's thinking, so that predominantly pessimistic ideas come to mind. People are more likely to engage in self-blame and feelings of hopelessness. This pessimistic style increases the likelihood of more long-term, serious depression.[34]

As you think about preaching to depressed listeners (and every congregation has more than a few), how can you encourage them to focus their attention on God's goodness and grace instead of ruminating on what they lack (Phil. 4:8)? How does the gospel answer people's deepest psychological needs? What does it take to free people from their fears and sadness and release them to a joy of living in the presence of God? In short, how can they experience the glorious liberty of the children of God in which they are called to "stand fast" (Gal. 5:1)? In what way does the gospel replace hopelessness with true and lasting hope? While some depressions have somatic roots and must be treated as physiological illnesses, all depressions can benefit from the sound psychology of applying Scripture with sensitivity and skill. It appears that men and women may generally handle stress and depression in different ways. At the same time, we all can handle life better as we come to know and trust God more deeply so that we can love him with our entire souls.

Communication Patterns and a Woman's Soul

In chapter 2, the importance of relationships to women was explored in the context of moral decision-making. Now the issue of relationship becomes central to understanding psychological differences between men and women.

For many women, the way men and women relate to one another appears to create self-esteem problems. One significant area of interaction lies in the vital task of communication. Various studies in the field of communication[35] point to differences in women's and men's communication patterns, although these scholars often disagree about both the size and nature of these differences and about the frequency with which they occur.[36]

Stereotypes may influence the impressions people have about men's and women's communication patterns. For example, the stereotype is that women talk more than men do, chatting interminably on the telephone or with a neighbor. Some studies found, however, that men typically talk more than women do.[37] Other studies indicated that men are more likely than women to use "filled pauses" (comments such as umm or uh) in order to "hold the floor" in a conversation without being interrupted.[38]

Differences also appear in other communication areas. One study found that when men speak, a higher proportion of their sentences are statements. When women speak, a higher proportion of their sentences are questions.[39] The researchers interpreted this as meaning that women need to lead off with a question, almost as if they must ask for permission to speak. They observed that when a woman speaks in a mixed group of men and women, she often enters with a question, in a deferential posture. Another study reported that women are more likely than men to hedge their remarks by adding disclaimers to them: "In my opinion . . . " "Personally, I think . . ." "I may be wrong, but . . ."[40] Some see this as an indication that women find it more difficult than men to state an opinion straightforwardly. A substantial number of studies[41] indicated that women's language style across the board is more self-deprecating than that of men and that women appear to be more hesitant and doubtful of their own credibility than are men. On the other hand, some writers argue that this female style is not actually self-deprecating but more "open" and "relational" than the typically more clipped masculine mode of speaking.[42] It is all too easy to make too much of the differences in patterns of communication (type-A error). At the same time, it is noteworthy that speaking styles appear to differ in these ways.

What is becoming clearer is that the social context of any interaction between men and women is decisive in explaining what appear to be gender differences. Both men and women use more expressive language in intimate conversations and more forceful language in formal settings. Change the setting and both men and women change the way they speak.[43] Furthermore, the fact that both men and women can learn patterns of communication that differ from those typical for their gender is further evidence that communication patterns are not fixed by gender. All of this is simply to say that while much has been written in the popular press on communication differences between men and women, most responsible studies provide little support for some of the popular myths of communication differences.[44]

All communication—verbal and nonverbal—resembles traffic controls on a busy street. Stop lights and stop signs determine who has the right-of-way and under what conditions. The right-of-way in communication is virtually always given to the person with higher status.[45] Many of the noted differences between the ways in which men and women communicate come from the power relations between them. The communication controls that individuals use depend not primarily on gender but on the status rankings of the people involved. Gender plays a role in setting the rules for communication, but gender in most cases appears to be an indirect force. It is the interaction between gender and social status that is decisive.

The Psychological Effects of Stereotyping

Stereotypes about status emerge in various ways. In one study, subjects were shown pictures of people sitting on two sides and one end of a rectangular table.[46] For each picture the question was the same: Who is the leader of this group? When the people at the table were all men or all women, the person sitting at the head of the table was chosen as the leader. This was also true when the group was mixed and a man was at the head of the table. But when both men and women were seated on the sides and a woman was at the head, many subjects chose a man on the side of the table as the leader rather than the woman sitting at the head.

Status is not the only factor affected by stereotypes. Several decades ago, Inge Broverman published the results of a classic study of stereotypes for men and women. In that study, mental health clinicians were given a list of 122 character traits. Some of the clinicians were asked to choose the characteristics that best described a mature, healthy adult *man*. Others were asked to choose the characteristics of a mature, healthy adult *woman*. Still others were asked to choose the characteristics of a mature, healthy *adult,* sex unspecified.

The results of this study showed a high correlation between the lists for a healthy adult *man* and a healthy *adult*. But the correlation between the healthy adult *woman* and a healthy *adult* was much lower. A woman, in the thinking of these mental health professionals, could not be a healthy *woman* and a healthy *adult* at the same time because a healthy adult rating corresponded to masculine characteristics.

The psychotherapists in this study declared women mentally healthy only if they conformed to the culturally accepted picture of the stereotypical woman: passive, dependent, childlike, accepting of her biologically inferior status. In recent decades, many mental health professionals have become aware of their bias and have worked to change it. Much of the popular literature in and out of the church, however, still reflects the same heavily dichotomized way of thinking about men and women. Thus, many psychotherapists (including Christian counselors) continue to work to produce passive, dependent women who accept their subordinate position without protest. This dichotomy reflects the powerful influence of Sigmund Freud's view of gender.

The following table shows a few of the most frequently selected character traits on the Broverman list of male and female characteristics placed in opposition to one another:

Stereotyped Characteristics of Men and Women

Men	Women
aggressive	unaggressive
unemotional	emotional
logical	illogical
rough	gentle
blunt	tactful
direct	sneaky
ambitious	unambitious
active	passive
independent	dependent
sloppy	neat

From Virginia Sapiro, *Women in American Society* (Palo Alto, Calif.: Mayfield Publishing, 1986), 260.

This table reflects the polarized stereotypes that are often seen as biologically based differences between men and women. But a number of readers will look at this list and say, "This description of a man (or woman) doesn't fit me at all." Such a narrow list does not begin to reflect the wonderful, wide, funny (and sometimes frustrating) range of behaviors that characterize human beings. We all know men who are neat and women who are sloppy. We know women who are logical and men who are illogical. And intuitively we understand that virtually all of us are some combination of both lists—at times we are active and at other times we are passive. We may be blunt in one situation and tactful in another. The list does not describe the reality of either our personhood or our life experience. But in a way that warps thinking and complicates the preaching task, this narrow, oversimplified dichotomy continues to define in many people's minds "the way we (men and women) are."

What happens to men and women when they are forced to live under this kind of stereotyping? Everyone loses—men, women, and God as well. The God-given potential of men and women is warped, constricted, distorted, even destroyed. It is not possible for men or women to become all God intended for them to be if their lives are defined by stereotypes rather than by a response to God's Word. This is evident in *Real Boys: Rescuing Our Sons from the Myths of Boyhood,* in which the author, William Pollack, reports a sense of isolation, alienation, despair, sadness, and disconnection that many men experience, though they cannot name or identify it.[47] To rob men of their more gentle, caring, and vulnerable side is as evil as robbing women of their active competency. The search to understand the possible relationship between levels of testosterone and aggressive behavior in men has often attracted public attention. It is less well known that there is considerable evidence that testosterone levels affect boys' behavior less than the ways in which they were loved, nurtured, and shaped by their parents and society.[48]

Stereotypical behaviors characterized by the traits listed in the Broverman study may contribute to problems in a number of areas. For example, how do the traits identified as "women's characteristics" affect women's responses to stress or women's high rate of utilization of counseling services? For many women, dealing with stress by straightforwardly seeking to change the situation may not be possible if they have been taught that women cannot actively initiate change but can only respond passively. For many women, self-competency plummets when they are trained to think that they are intuitive rather than logical and that they are dependent (and thus cannot act independently). It is not difficult to see that stereotypical gender education might contribute to the high rate at which women seek the help of counselors.

Some people think that women are the primary consumers of counseling services in North America because women are more willing to seek help. Our culture gives women permission to be sick in ways that are not true for men. We expect men to be strong and in control, whereas women have cultural permission to admit that they have problems. Others suggest that women may seek counseling more often than men do because it is culturally acceptable for a woman to be dependent on someone else—a therapist, in this case. She can assume the role of the weak, submissive client, a role that is much more difficult for a man to assume in our culture.[49]

But when women's use of counseling services is examined more closely, it becomes apparent that it is not women per se but certain groups of women who comprise the majority of those seeking counseling. Within-group differences show up in one study that looks at the ratio of men to women who sought psychiatric help. Married women were more likely than men to get psychiatric treatment, but widowed, never married, separated, or divorced women were *less* likely than men to seek and receive psychiatric treatment.[50] (When single individuals are compared, the single man is more likely to seek counseling.)[51] This underlines women's marital status as a factor to be examined. Women's *biology* alone does not seem to account for the difference. Married women sought and received treatment in greater numbers than did men, but men outnumbered widowed, never married, separated, or divorced women in seeking therapeutic treatment.[52]

Furthermore, R. Helson and J. Picano found that women at midlife who had followed a traditional life plan (exclusively as homemakers) tended to have more chronic physical conditions and less energy than their female peers with less traditional life plans (including a mix of homemaking and career).[53] Francis Purifoy and Lambert Koopmans found that "working married women complain of fewer symptoms [of] . . . stress [i.e., headaches, insomnia, depression, anxiety] than housewives. . . . Among those women who work outside the home, traditional women's jobs [i.e., clerical, sales, and service work] are the most stressful for women in terms of mental health and heart disease."[54] Such women are more likely to "experience nervous breakdowns, to suffer from depression, nervousness, insomnia, and nightmares, and to be in psychotherapy."[55] When mental health researchers G. L. Klerman and M. M. Weissman reviewed all the literature on depression research in women and tested for factors ranging from genetics to PMS to birth control pills, they found only two prime factors for female depression: low social status and/or marriage.[56]

Thus, many women (Christian women included) live with debilitating issues of low self-esteem and depression, both potentially compounded by stereotypes and both influencing how they deal with stress. Christian women bring those issues to church with them each week. Should these issues make any difference in the way pastors preach? Or because differences *among* women and *among* men are also evident, does this mean that the research can be ignored? Issues such as low self-esteem, depression, or a passivity that precludes dealing effectively with stress all form lenses through which women see or fail to see what the preacher hopes to communicate from the pulpit.

How Does This Apply to Preaching?

Haddon Robinson states that the first question an exegete should ask of any passage of Scripture is, What is the vision of God in this text? The second question is, What is the "depravity factor" in the text—what is the sin issue here?[57] In subtle but powerful ways, the impact of gender stereotypes on women in the pew is part of the depravity factor. As noted earlier in this chapter, gender stereotypes can heighten stress if a woman does not know that she can act to change stressful situations. Gender stereotypes can cause women to bury their gifts and even deny a part of God's call in their lives because they believe a stereotype of what they ought to be. As you exegete a biblical text, ask yourself about the depravity factor, the sin issue, that may keep people from loving God with all their souls. Are there stereotypes that need to be destroyed by truth from God's Word because they keep women from being all that God created them to be?

As you preach, you must also face the impact of stereotypes on yourself. What do *you* think it means to be a man or a woman? How does this come through in your preaching? Robert Howard asks, "If all the actors in a preacher's stories are strong, healthy, cheery white males, what does that imply for those who do *not* possess those attributes? Are they banished to the bleachers of life, confined solely to watching the 'real Christians' go about the business of God?"[58] The illustrations, examples, stories, and metaphors you use to make sermon points convey more about yourself than you may realize. Citing the first five sermons in one issue of *Pulpit Digest,*[59] Howard noted that of the twenty-four images used by the preachers, only two contained women in active roles and two portrayed both men and women as actors. Twenty of the first twenty-four images used only men as examples. He concludes, "Theologically, the exclusion of women's point of view in the imagery of sermons distorts the very Good News that preachers seek to proclaim."[60] If women as well as men are to love God with all their souls, they will find powerful help to do so in biblical examples, illustrations, stories, and metaphors of women as well as men who are psychologically whole.

For example, women who do not know that they can take action to change bad situations do well to hear of Abigail (1 Samuel 25). She was married to an evil man, Nabal, who acted stupidly toward those to whom he had a debt. When his actions provoked David to organize a full-scale military action against Nabal's household, quick-thinking Abigail headed off the trouble that threatened the lives of everyone under her roof. In going against her husband's wishes, she saved his life. She changed a stressful situation rather than merely wringing her hands about it. Or take the story of Leah (Genesis 29–30), a woman married to a man who did not love her. Watch her do everything in her power (unsuccessfully) to earn her husband's love. But also look at the progression in her mind and heart as she named each of her six sons. This woman could not change her stressful situation, but she could change the meaning of it as she came to focus not on what she lacked (Jacob's love) but on what God had given her (six sons). She could be psychologically whole even without the love of her husband. It is difficult to name many problems people face today that were not faced and overcome by women in the biblical narratives.[61]

Preaching can subtly reinforce gender stereotypes unless you bring to the pulpit a clear vision not only of God and of human depravity but also of a godly, healthy human being created in God's image. Without that as an integral part of preaching, women cannot learn to love God with all their souls. The preacher's vision of what constitutes a godly, healthy person powerfully shapes the message given and the message heard.

As chapter 2 examined male and female differences in moral decision-making, it became clear that for many women, decision-making is dominated by the personal, by the impact of their decisions on other people. As the primary or only criterion for decision-making, this is dangerous and can lead to decisions that do not honor God. In contrast, many men's decision-making is guided exclusively by the impersonal or the legal. Jesus made it clear (Matthew 5) that law without attention to the context of its application leads to legalism. The call of Scripture is to moral decision-making that combines the two—that we do justice *and* love mercy (Micah 6:8). Just as preaching about moral questions must include both justice and mercy, so preaching about men and women must work from a vision of godly, healthy humanity uncontaminated by gender stereotypes.

An old cliche says that the preacher's task is to afflict the comfortable and to comfort the afflicted. People can be destroyed if we turn that around. By not being sensitive to the gender stereotypes that affect both men and women in our congregations, we can end up afflicting the afflicted. Those who are sons and daughters of the King of kings should see themselves as princes and princesses on the way to heaven.

Summing Up the Chapter

- Men and women tend to deal with stress differently because many women are taught that being passive is a proper female posture in life.

- A fundamental aim of preaching is to empower listeners to incorporate what they have heard from Scripture into solutions to the challenges of everyday life.
- Biblical self-esteem, while anchored in our acknowledgment that we are sinners continually in need of God's grace, also affirms our worth as those whom God has called and gifted. We are designed to serve God fully with the gifts he has given us.
- As you look for the vision of God and the depravity factor embedded in a biblical text, ask also about gender stereotypes that affect men and women in the pew.
- Women listeners need biblical examples, illustrations, stories, and metaphors of women who are psychologically whole.
- Preaching can subtly reinforce gender stereotypes unless you bring to the pulpit a clear vision of godly, healthy men and women who are psychologically whole. Without that vision, men and women cannot learn to love God with all their souls.

Questions to Ponder

- How can you preach so that both men and women are empowered to love God with all their souls?
- What do you (the preacher) think it means to be a psychologically whole man or woman?
- How important (or trivial) does it seem to you that your sermons include positive examples of women as well as men as illustrations of your points? Why is that important (or trivial)?

4

How Do We Know What We Know?

As a growing child, then as a teenager, I struggled with issues of faith and doubt. Everyone around me seemed sure and secure as Christians while I lay awake night after night trying to fathom God. If the pastor said anything about faith in his sermon, I would sit up and listen carefully for some kind of explanation of God and of trust that I could get my mind around. But during those years, rarely did any of the many preachers to whom I listened (at Bible conferences as well as at our church) address my issues. It seemed that I was alone in the church with the overwhelming doubts that tormented me. When I was sixteen, a friend loaned me his copy of G. Campbell Morgan's book *The Triumphs of Faith*. I devoured it, looking for a reasonable reason to "believe" that God is and that he rewards those who diligently seek him (Heb. 11:6). The book did not answer all my questions, but at least it kept me from bolting out the backdoor of the church.

The Great Commandment states that we are to love God not only with all our hearts and with all our souls but also with all our *minds* (Matt. 22:37). How can you help your people love God with all their minds? Should you focus on preaching rational explanations of the Christian faith? I remember memorizing the rational proofs for the existence of God when I was in college, but the proofs did not help me to *love* God, only to fear him. No, preaching to help people love God with all their minds is more complex than merely discussing why it is reasonable to believe in God or even in his goodness and love.

What makes preaching even more challenging is that congregations bring together people who do not all think alike. I felt alone with my doubts in my church during my growing-up years. Despite the diversity of many congregations, you may have few, if any, "chronic doubters" like me to deal with as you preach each week, but whether or not you face doubters each time you stand in the pulpit, you must know that there are many ways of "knowing" truth. That brings us to the various ways of knowing that men and women bring to church each Sunday, the many ways of knowing that you face each time you stand up to preach God's truth.

Epistemology is the study of how people know what they know. Because this is a large subject, crucial to the preaching task, chapters 4, 5, and 6 of this book focus on aspects of epistemology that affect preaching to women. We do not often think of people being preoccupied with the question of how they know what they know. In fact, we ourselves seldom ask how we know what we know. But it is a question tied to other profound and difficult questions such as What is truth? or What is authority? or To whom should I listen? or What counts for me as evidence?[1]

Such questions touch the very core of what preaching is about. How we shape what we say in the pulpit consciously or unconsciously deals with these questions.[2] They have to do with our basic assumptions about the nature of truth and reality and with the origins of knowledge. Our epistemologies shape the way we see the world and see ourselves living in our world. They affect our definition of ourselves and the way we interact with others. They affect our public and private personae, our sense of control over life events, and our view of teaching and learning. How we know what we know also affects our conceptions of morality.

While our epistemologies shape the way we see the world, they are themselves shaped by our family backgrounds and our ongoing life experiences. Although our ways of knowing truth are remarkably stable, these patterns of thinking are not ours in a closed system. We are not locked into a single way of knowing throughout a lifetime. For this reason, investigators have attempted to observe people over long periods of time in order to understand and describe how people's patterns of identifying truth may change.

Epistemological Differences between Men and Women

Until fairly recently, women have been omitted from many major studies leading to the formation of psychological theories. Studies were done on men, and then if women were considered at all, researchers looked for ways in which women differed from or conformed to male patterns. (Kohlberg's research, described in chapter 2, is a good example.) As a result, characteristics traditionally associated with men were valued, studied, and articulated—things such as the development of autonomy and independence, abstract critical thought, and the development of a morality based on rights and justice. Much less research has focused on the development of more "feminine" characteristics such as interdependence, intimacy, nurturing, and contextual thought.[3] Men's experience served as the baseline, and wherever women differed, they were considered inferior. For this reason, we must be cautious when considering the nature of what may appear to be gender-based differences between the thinking of men and women. The language used to describe "thinking" has become entangled in our stereotyped understanding of men and women. Go back and look again at the traits in the Broverman study (chap. 3): To "think" is to be male; to "feel" is to be female. If a woman comes to believe the stereotype, how can she, a woman, know truth in the context of this thinking/feeling dichotomy?

The dichotomy identified in the Broverman study simply reflected the practice long inherent in the study of intellectual development. Mental processes involving abstract impersonal "operations" were labeled "thinking." The mental processes involving the personal and interpersonal "operations" were called "emotional." A hundred years ago or more, it was assumed that a person could not develop an equal capacity and ability both to think and to feel. This belief led those in authority throughout the nineteenth century to exclude women from the academic community. Physicians of the time were clear about the "fact" that if women engaged in intellectual pursuits, their reproductive organs would shrivel up and become unusable.[4] This either-or thinking about mental and emotional life led people to conclude, erroneously, that if an individual expended energy thinking, he or she would inevitably deplete his or her capacity for emotion, and vice versa. The wisdom of the time both in academia and on the street was that women's *intellectual* development would inhibit their emotional capacity to nurture and love, whereas men's *emotional* development would impair their intellectual functioning. A person could not develop both and therefore should not try to do so.

In the context of this widespread belief, in the 1950s and 1960s, William Perry conducted a longitudinal study that provided a benchmark for studying how we know what we know.[5] Given the beliefs and research practices of the time, it is not surprising that he chose to work with only male students at Harvard University. In his research with these men, Perry followed their cognitive or epistemological development over time, and he identified four categories or patterns of thinking through which these men knew what they believed was truth. In studying these men, Perry concluded that there was a sequence of developmental growth through these categories that characterized the experience of these men.[6]

When women were assessed on Perry's scale, however, they did not quite fit the norms he had established. It became evident that a similar study of women's cognition was called for. In the late 1970s and early 1980s, four women psychologists examined the development of self, mind, and voice in women.[7] They concluded that women's ways of knowing could be analyzed with somewhat different categories. At the risk of oversimplifying the work of both Perry and Mary Belenky and her colleagues, I have laid their schemas side by side in the following chart. This layout could imply an apples-to-apples comparison, which would not be accurate. There were important differences in the research methods used. Perry's study covered a longer period of time and focused on a select group of male undergraduates at Harvard University. The Belenky study lasted less than five years and focused on not only university women but also a wider group that included women on public assistance and women in counseling. While the categories overlap in some ways, they are not identical and should not be considered so.

William Perry Study of Male Harvard Undergraduates	Mary Belenky et al. Study of a Diverse Group of Women
There were no men in this category.	*Silence:* These women experience themselves as mindless and voiceless.
Basic dualism: These men are passive learners who believe everything in the world is either right or wrong, good or evil.	*Received knowers:* These women, who are also dualists, do not believe they can create knowledge on their own.
Multiplicity: These men believe that many issues are matters of taste or personal preference, not issues of right and wrong.	*Subjective knowers:* These women reject external authorities and conceive of knowledge as something personal, private, and subjectively known.
Relativism subordinate: These men cultivate an analytical approach to knowledge, looking for evidence.	*Procedural knowers:* These women invest in learning and in applying objective procedures for learning.
Full relativism: For these men, truth is relative in all areas of life, and meaning depends on the context of an event.	*Constructed knowers:* These women value both subjective and objective strategies for knowing.

How Important Are Differing Gender Patterns in How We Know What We Know?

If we lay the two systems side by side as in the above table, the first category describes women who do not know that they are able to know anything at all. (No men were in this category in Perry's study.)[8] Such women experience themselves as mindless and voiceless, subject to the whims of more powerful people outside themselves.[9] Women who live in silence believe they are not capable of knowing anything and that the most important thing they can do is to attach themselves to people who do know and can tell them what they need to know. These women assume that only men really know things. They live in silence, submitting to the authority figures in their lives. They do not speak out because they assume they are too stupid to have anything of value to say. This is an extreme denial of self and an extreme dependence on external authorities for direction in every area of life. You may know women like this in your congregation.

For the women in this category of the Belenky study, words spoken to them were viewed as weapons being used against them. People use words to separate and diminish people, not to connect and empower them. The silent women worried that they would be punished just for using words—any words. While these women had words and could speak to interviewers, they could not explore the usefulness of words for expressing or developing thought. These women were passive, reactive, and dependent. They saw authorities as all-powerful because of the authorities' physical strength or positional power, not because of their expertise. These women were convinced that blind obedience to authorities was necessary for staying out of trouble and for ensuring their own survival.

The second category in the women's study parallels the first category in the men's study.[10] Both the men and the women in this category are passive knowers who tend to view everything as either good or bad, right or wrong, with no middle ground. According to the Belenky study, a person with this way of knowing has the following characteristics:

1. Ideas and ideals are concrete and dualistic: Things are right or wrong, true or false, good or bad. Every question has only one right answer because there are no gray areas or gradations.
2. All truth is absolute, and the only way to know what is true is to locate and listen to the right authority figure. These knowers are completely dependent on external authority figures because they do not believe it is possible for them to construct knowledge in their own heads.
3. For these passive knowers, a paradox is inconceivable because several contradictory ideas cannot agree with the facts simultaneously.
4. They cannot tolerate ambiguity. They are literal. Although they collect facts, they do not develop their own opinions.
5. They want predictability (what will happen when) and clarity (what is expected of them).
6. Their moral judgments conform to the conventions of their particular society, and they strive to subordinate their own wishes or actions to the voices of others.
7. They perceive that developing their own powers is always at the expense of others. If a woman chooses to excel, those she loves will be penalized in some way. Thus, she must choose the welfare of others over her own.
8. Such women typically approach adulthood understanding that the selfless care and empowerment of others is central to their life's work and to their personal survival.
9. Even self-knowledge comes from others. These women organize attempts at self-definition around external social expectations that define concrete social and occupational roles for them.[11]

Take a closer look at a few of these points. According to the Perry and Belenky studies, the first five are characteristic of both men and women, but from the sixth characteristic onward, men and women differ. Only the women are characterized by the development of the "selfless self." Because the received-knower category emphasizes dualism (only two options exist for anything), these women assume that in any conflict between the self and the claims of others, they must choose one or the other. They cannot choose both. Women in this category of knowing worry that if they choose to develop their own gifts, abilities, or powers, doing so will inevitably be at the expense of others. They accept that the world is hierarchically arranged and dualistic: A person is a leader or a follower, a shepherd or a member of the flock, a speaker or a listener. Some of our cultural standards dictate that women should be listeners, followers, subordinate, and unassertive. These women fear diminishing others by acting on their own behalf because their deepest identities center on being nice, caring for others, and refraining from inflicting hurt.

The final distinctive characteristic (identity formation) in the list above was true of the women in the Belenky study but not true of the men in Perry's study. Such women see themselves only as they are mirrored in the eyes of others. Consequently, they experience a great need to live up to other people's expectations in the hope of keeping others from taking a dim view of them. These women listen carefully and seek urgently to live up to the images that others have held up to them. They are particularly at the mercy of authorities who tell them that they are wrong or bad or crazy. Many women can shut down their intellectual powers almost completely if told they are dumb, incompetent, or should not step outside certain boundaries.

On the other hand, the authority who seeks out and praises the intelligence of women in this category may alter their way of seeing themselves. Authority figures hold considerable leverage and can be in particularly strategic positions to help these women find the ability, latent in their own minds, to think.

In contrast to the first group of women, who think they cannot know anything, women in the category of received or passive knowers believe that they know a great many things. But everything they accept as true comes from an outside authority figure. They know they look good because they consulted the best hairdresser to choose their hairstyle, a color analyst to tell them what colors to wear, and a personal shopper to help them pick out their clothes. They know their homes look good because an interior decorator told them what to buy and where to put it. Christian women in this category often know a great deal about the Bible because they put themselves under the authorities who can tell them what the Bible says and what it means. Many Christian received knowers faithfully attend church and Bible study groups, especially if the studies are taught by highly respected authority figures. But these women do not believe they are capable of generating facts and ideas through reflection on their own experiences. As a result, they are certain that the only true and dependable knowledge they have comes from the outside authorities they have accepted.

The leaders of some churches encourage parishioners to question and discuss with others what is taught. The leaders of other churches encourage parishioners to accept what is taught without question. The stance of a particular church often depends on its leaders' view of authority: Does authority rest in the teacher, in the teaching itself, or in the Word on which the teaching is based? If authority rests in the teacher, then listeners are encouraged to accept what is said without questioning it. If authority rests in the Word, then listeners may be encouraged to interact with the Word for themselves. In the thinking of some leaders, however, such interaction may open the door to unacceptable alternative interpretations. Thus, they reinforce the authority of the teacher. As a result, in many churches, a large number of laymen and women are received or passive knowers. They may read the Bible faithfully, but they are quite sure they will not *really* understand it until the pastor explains it to them.[12] If such listeners do not understand the explanation, they do not blame the pastor; they blame themselves. As a result, a preacher may never know that he or she is not communicating with them.

What happens when a woman who has put her trust in an authority figure later finds that her trust was badly misplaced?[13] The Belenky study of women's ways of knowing found that for some women, that crisis of trust pushed them into a different (third) way of knowing. They shifted from trusting in the knowledge others could give them (i.e., receiving from others as received knowers) to rejecting all knowledge from outside authorities and trusting only what they could know in their own minds (as subjective knowers).[14] They came to a point of believing that they could *not* trust what they had been told by external authorities. They concluded that nothing they had been taught was trustworthy.

In this five-year research project, more than half the women who moved into this third way of knowing (as subjective knowers) had recently taken steps to end relationships with husbands or lovers, and they rejected any further obligations to family members and moved away on their own. Belenky and her colleagues concluded:

> There were almost no women in this group who were not actively and obsessively preoccupied with a choice between self and other, acting on behalf of [the] self as opposed to denying the self and living for and through others.[15]

For these women, their epistemological shift produced a complete reversal, a 180-degree turn. For Perry's men, his second category (multiplicity) merely added to what was already there. For the women in the Belenky study, however, their sense of outrage and deception was so strong that in response they rejected all external authorities in their lives.

M. Gay Hubbard recounts a moment of truth that may help us understand this shift. She recalls a college general psychology class during which the students were observing two wiggly vertical lines on a sheet of paper:

> I remember the professor saying in his highly directive teaching style, "Now, see a vase; now, change and see the faces," and as a good, obedient sophomore I did as I was told. It was not until I was wandering back to the library that it occurred to me that I had learned *two* things, both of which were important—only one of which, however, had been pointed out by my professor. First, I had learned that I could decide what I would see. Second, the point my professor neglected to discuss, I had learned that someone could tell me what to see. While thinking about this second discovery, it occurred to me that at the point I was told what to see, I had an additional, crucial choice: I could choose to see as I was told, or choose my own point of view.[16]

Over the last three decades in women's ministries, I have spent countless hours listening to women who, after years of seeing only what they were told to see, discovered that they could choose their own point of view. In the process, they walked away from marriages lasting twenty-five years or more, including in some cases marriage to Christian leaders. Some of these women are classic textbook cases of a shift in epistemology, suddenly dumping everything they had previously embraced. In their anger and frustration, they have said to me, "They [the church or pastor or teacher] lied to me! They told me that if I did it all according to the Bible, I'd be happy. They were wrong. They lied to me!"

If you minister to a group that includes a significant number of women, it is possible that the group includes a few women who right now may be in the process of making this epistemological shift. The problem is that you are not likely to know the shift is happening until after it has taken place. Where do these women, who feel the authorities they have been taught to trust have lied to them, turn for truth? Women who choose to disrupt all relationships by walking away have, for the most part, decided that truth is found only within their own experience.

Most of us would agree that it is indeed unusual when a woman walks away from her marriage and family and possibly even hitchhikes to San Francisco to become a hooker! Yet such an event has a trigger—or many triggers over a long period of time. A woman does not make this shift in a vacuum. When this happens in the lives of Christian women—often with long histories of commitment and service to Christ—we need to look more closely at the triggers that prompt such drastic action.

When women are not encouraged to study and think for themselves, or when they are led to believe that only men can think, they are cut off from developing their own minds, their own critical faculties. And if they choose authority figures who in some way let them down, what resources do they have to handle the situation? It is dangerous to encourage mental or intellectual passivity in anyone in the church. People who are not encouraged to study and learn for themselves may one day discover that they can choose to see what they are told to see, or they can choose their own point of view. In that process, they may choose to walk away from their families, from the church, and from God. When that happens, we need to ask ourselves why—and how we can keep that from happening in our churches or in our homes.

How Does This Apply to Preaching?

As students of preaching know well, a preacher can do only three things with an idea: explain it, prove it, and apply it. Turned around, these are the three functional questions budding preachers are taught to ask in sermon preparation: What does the text mean? Is it true? So what?[17] A great many preachers think it is enough to deal in the weekly sermon with the first functional question: What does it mean? The preaching stance is that of the authoritative teacher explaining what the text says. This stance strongly encourages men and women to sit in the pew as passive learners.

In recent years, some preachers have given more attention to the third functional question: So what? This is the question of application:

How does this apply to our lives?[18] It is the second functional question that preachers most often ignore: Is it true? (This was my central question as a teenager.) Yet it is this question raised in a sermon that draws listeners into a more active use of their minds as they listen. C. S. Lewis was a master of the use of the second functional question: He could raise objections to an assertion in such a way that, like reading a good detective novel, the reader would sit back and say, "Hmmm, yeah, how can the writer get around that point?"[19] It is precisely this functional question that pushes people to use their minds more actively as they listen to sermons.

Yet it is easy for preachers to stay with the first functional question and thus encourage a passive-knower stance in their listeners. On Sunday mornings, such listeners are attentive, perhaps even taking notes on what the preacher says. This may be flattering to the preacher, but there are major problems in encouraging this posture in Christians. Let me illustrate one danger.

Political scientist and historian Samuel Huntington has described four ways in which people respond to the strain they may experience when an ideal they have embraced stands in sharp contrast to their lived reality.[20] While Huntington wrote about strain on the national political scene in different eras, his insights can be applied equally well to any situation in which an ideal and a reality are at odds. He developed the following table to help us understand the ways people handle such a gap between their ideal and their reality:

	Perception of Gap	
Intensity of belief in ideals	Clear	Unclear
High	Moralism (eliminate gap)	Hypocrisy (deny gap)
Low	Cynicism (tolerate gap)	Complacency (ignore gap)

From Samuel P. Huntington, *American Politics: The Promise of Disharmony* (Cambridge: Harvard University Press, 1981), 64.

Let me apply Huntington's table to the case of received-knower women in the church today, to women who will sit in the pew next week and listen to you preach. Let's suppose that these Christian women have listened to you in the past, have believed what you have told them, and have jotted down notes in their Bibles to help them remember what you have said. Let's further suppose that somewhere along the line, you have created in their minds an *ideal* for their lives, accompanied by promises from the Bible that assure them of a good reward for living up to the ideal. For example, let me assume that at some time you have preached on Philippians 4:6–7:

> Be anxious for nothing, but in everything by prayer and supplication, with thanksgiving, let your requests be made known to God; and the peace of God, which surpasses all understanding, will guard your hearts and minds through Christ Jesus.

You will bring your own understanding to that text. But a person in the pew reading the text might assume, "It is possible to live with tranquillity, with a peace that passes all understanding, simply by praying about my needs." The *ideal* is peace. The *means* is prayer.

So what happens when a woman in the third row prays fervently every day but is still gnawed by anxiety? She can react to that reality in any one of the following four ways:

1. She can believe fervently in the ideal of peace in exchange for prayer but remain unclear about the way the ideal relates to her experience (upper right quadrant). She has a strong belief in the ideal, but her perception of the gap between her experience and the ideal is unclear, and her discomfort with the gap is vague. She is likely to react in one of two ways: She may hypocritically deny the gap to others, or she may deny the gap to herself. Denying her experience of worry because she now prays daily, she says that she has peace in spite of her ongoing anxiety.
2. But suppose this woman has a weak belief in the ideal of peace along with an unclear perception of the gap between the ideal and her personal experience (lower right quadrant). In this case, she will likely become complacent. She will pray because Christians are supposed to pray. But to herself she may say, "This peace thing really isn't possible in the twenty-first century. Maybe it worked in Paul's day, but he didn't live now and couldn't possibly know how frantic American life is today. Besides, with violence in the streets and drugs in the schools, peace is an impossible goal. Praying can't hurt, but don't get excited about peace. It won't happen." When individuals accept the ideal only casually and lack a sharp sense of the gap between their experience and the ideal, they

are likely to choose to ignore the gap with some complacency. The ideal does not hold great meaning or appeal.

3. But suppose the woman's perception of the gap is clear. In that case, her responses to the passage will be very different. Perhaps she hears you preach about peace from Philippians 4:6–7 and decides that peace would be wonderful to have. She looks at her life and sees clearly that she does not have peace (she is clear about the gap). But she also may not *believe* you when you say that the ideal of peace is possible. In that case, she is likely to set aside the message with some cynicism (lower left quadrant). She is clear about the gap, but she does not really believe in the ideal (as nice as it would be to have it). Several things can trigger this cynicism. Suppose she has been promised other things from the pulpit that she took to heart. She went after them in the past, but nothing came of her efforts. She thought she did what you said to do, but it did not work. She might conclude that you really don't know what you're talking about. Or she may look at your frazzled life and say, "If that's peace, I don't want it." Cynicism can have many roots, but regardless of where it comes from, the result is the same: The woman stops believing you and what you say.
4. But suppose the woman hears you preach on Philippians 4:6–7 and loves what you tell her about peace in exchange for prayer. You convince her that it is really possible to have peace, so she begins to pray every day, turning everything over to God. She wants desperately to reduce the tension or the gap between the ideal and her personal reality (upper left quadrant). In the process, she develops what Huntington called "moral passion." She wants to achieve the ideal because she has come to believe in the ideal and she knows she does not have it. This conviction puts at least one of several actions in motion:

    - She goes after peace with all her heart, convinced that if she does everything you tell her, it will be hers. If she reaches the goal, her faith in you, in your word, in God, and in God's Word is reinforced, and her life is enriched.
    - But suppose peace does *not* come. She will then begin to question your authority, wondering how she can be sure you are right.

- Her urgency to have this peace grows. She asks herself, "Why isn't this peace my personal experience? What needs to change?"
- If she still does not have the peace you promised her, her questions about your personal authority expand and she begins attacking the church you represent, thinking that the church lied, the church is wrong.
- When she reaches that point, she begins to question all social conventions and may experiment with alternatives.[21]

At this point, the sincere believer makes an epistemological shift. She may be lost to your congregation and possibly to the kingdom of Christ.

Of these four responses to what you have preached, with which one are you most comfortable? Ideally, pastors want their people to have moral passion, but pragmatically, they may be more comfortable with some level of complacency. The risks are much lower. The promises made explicitly or implicitly by pastors are taken very seriously by some people in the pews. Therefore, do not promise more than you can deliver.

When you step before an audience, tell the truth. Do not make up fairy tales about the Christian life. People are listening, and they may hear and take seriously what you say. Do not promise more than the gospel promises: The gospel of Jesus Christ promises deliverance from spiritual death and hell. The gospel promises eternal life with the eternal God. The gospel promises God's empowering presence in our lives. But the gospel does not promise that if we live a certain way, certain results are 100 percent guaranteed. A woman being battered by her deacon- or elder-husband should not be told that if she is submissive, she will have a wonderful, fulfilling marriage. Her marriage is a torment, and she may end up in a coffin if her husband's violence escalates.[22]

In your preaching, do not gloss over the problems women face in bad marriages. Do not dismiss the struggle of single mothers, the stress and hassle of the work world, the painful obligations posed by aging parents. Do not ignore or trivialize women's realities. When you do, you may help push them toward disillusionment with the church and with the gospel.

Over the years I have seen too many women walk away from the church and from God, women who once were deeply committed to the Christian ideal and were clear about the gap between their personal experiences and the promises held out to them in the church. They developed moral passion, which led them to do everything in their power to make the ideal come true in their lives. When that did not happen, they left the church and the faith.

Max Weber, considered to be the father of sociology of religion, wrote that "the sacred is the uniquely unalterable."[23] Whatever you stamp as *sacred* by your words from the pulpit, you also stamp as *unalterable* for many listeners. So when you say, "Thus saith the Lord!" be sure that your words accurately reflect what God has said. It is dangerous to say in God's name what God has not said. When women take your words seriously as the very words of God, and then they discover that your prescription does not cure their ills, they question not only you but the One in whose name you speak.

Of course, not all passive knowers experience a crisis in their lives that pushes them to reject all external authorities in their lives. Many remain passive knowers throughout their lives. Others move to different ways of knowing without the bumpy ride through crisis and rejection of truth presented by outside authorities. Chapter 5 continues to examine how people know what they know and looks at some of the issues involved in preaching to women with more flexible and interactive epistemologies. As you employ the second functional question (Is it true?) and thus encourage women to use their minds and to wrestle with the biblical text with you, you will open them to loving God with all their minds. You may also help them move to other ways of knowing that expand their capacity to love God with their whole being.

Summing Up the Chapter

- Women received knowers worry that if they choose to develop their own gifts, abilities, or powers, doing so will inevitably be at the expense of others. This fear of diminishing others by acting on their own behalf is intolerable because their deepest identities center on being nice, caring for others, and refraining from inflicting hurt.
- Many women can shut down their intellectual powers almost completely if told they are dumb, incompetent, or should not step outside certain boundaries.
- When women are not encouraged to study and think for themselves—when they are led to believe that only men can think—

they are cut off from developing their own minds, their own critical faculties. It is dangerous to encourage mental or intellectual passivity in anyone (male or female) in the church.

- Authorities hold considerable leverage and can be in particularly strategic positions to help passive knowers and dualistic thinkers find the power that may reside in their own minds.
- The second functional question (Is it true?) draws listeners into a more active use of their minds as they listen.
- Ideally, pastors want their people to have moral passion, but pragmatically, they may be more comfortable with some level of complacency. The risks are much lower.
- When you step before a congregation, do not make up fairy tales about the Christian life. Do not promise more than the gospel promises.
- Whatever you stamp as *sacred* by your words from the pulpit, you also stamp as *unalterable* for many listeners. When you say, "Thus saith the Lord!" be sure that your words accurately reflect what God has said. It is dangerous to say in God's name what God has not said.

Questions to Ponder

- What do you think might be different in men's and women's life experiences that could account for the differences in passive knowing or the rejection of external authorities seen in some women's ways of knowing?
- When you look at the church, what are the advantages of having passive knowers in the pews? What are the downsides of this?
- Does the fact that different members of your congregation bring different ways of knowing to church suggest to you any variations in the type of appeals you might make to them? Does one size fit all in effective preaching?
- Are there clues that would help you evaluate the ways of knowing in your congregation? How would you go about assessing the epistemological needs of your people?
- In light of this chapter, how can you preach so that your people, especially women, learn to love God with all their minds?

5

Modern and Postmodern Listeners

We live in "the best of times and the worst of times," to borrow a line from Charles Dickens.[1] We enjoy the comforts and efficiencies of our times at the same time that our culture invades our churches, bringing a host of pressures to tear us from God. How can we anchor ourselves to truth in the midst of change and those things that woo us from the eternal? This is every preacher's challenge every time God's Word is proclaimed from a pulpit. But often the message is fuzzy because we ourselves are so embedded in our culture that we cannot discern the difference between what lasts and what passes away. We may be seduced by the culture into valuing too highly what is merely temporal. And it is possible to be tempted to equate the temporal with the eternal, mistaking something cultural for what is biblically mandated.

As we continue examining epistemologies (how we know what we know) and how they relate to loving God with all our minds, we come to what may be considered "modern" and "postmodern" epistemologies. Those who speak in God's name must be clear about them and how they affect listeners, especially women listeners. Because we evangelicals love to bash postmodernism,[2] let me begin there and work back to modernism.

The term *postmodernism* has become a trash can for whatever many of us think we do not like or want to face. For my generation, the shift from clean to cluttered in everything from television commercials and magazine layouts to the mishmash in clothing or home decor sets our teeth on edge. Glitzy television commercials blast us with a kaleidoscope of images bouncing on top of one another, giving us no time to sort them out or understand how they relate. We blanch at the funky baggy clothes and styles that reject coherence and beauty, even though we know that postmodern design tells us we can mix anything with anything (more or less). If we are lured into a modern art gallery, we question how scraps raided from a junkyard and welded together into an indecipherable "sculpture" can possibly be called art. We may get the point of the fragmentation and juxtaposition in Picasso's *Guernica,* but would anyone really consider a painting of Brillo boxes or Campbell's soup cans "art"?

When we as Christians think of postmodernism, we often connect it to the absence of values and truth in American society today. We hear people say, "That may be true for you, but it isn't true for me"—whether they are referring to a biblical doctrine we hold dear or to an ethical value such as truthfulness or fidelity that we take for granted.

In recent years as I have talked with leaders of ministries to women, they have assured me that they know how to teach modern women, but they are not sure how to teach postmodern women. So when we think about preaching in a postmodern world, the prospect seems pretty bleak. Who will believe our gospel? Who will follow the disciplined road to a deep relationship with God? When all truth is spelled in the lowercase, denying the possibility of capital-T Truth, how can we preach Jesus Christ as the way, the truth, and the life and get a hearing?

Part of the discomfort some of us feel when it comes to preaching to postmodern women may be due to the fact that we see ourselves as completely out of touch with many of the values and ideas that characterize our postmodern world. Let's step back into history for a short tour that may help us gain perspective on ministering in this world of ours.

How We Got Where We Are

Sociologists of religion continue to examine how a world that once was universally religious could, at least in Western Europe and North America, become almost completely secularized, as it is today. The early Christian creeds[3] described the church as "one, holy, *universal* [catholic], and apostolic," and in the period between Constantine and the Reformation, it seemed that, in fact, there was only one "face" of Western Christianity. Peter Berger depicts the immense network of saints, sacraments, mystery, miracle, and magic that held together the catholic universe of the Middle Ages. He likens this network to a tent held up by many poles. He then examines the impact on that world of the Reformation with its central emphasis on *sola Scriptura* and *sola gratia.* The Reformation not only created more than one "face" of Christianity to confuse laypeople and to ignite a hundred years of religious wars but also removed the panoply of mystery, miracle, and magic that had "mediated" between earth and heaven:

> The Protestant believer no longer lives in a world ongoingly penetrated by sacred beings and forces. Reality is polarized between a radically transcendent divinity and a radically "fallen" humanity that is devoid of sacred qualities. Between them lies an altogether "natural" universe, God's creation to be sure, but in itself bereft of numinosity. . . . The Catholic lives in a world in which the sacred is mediated . . . through a variety of channels—the sacraments of the church, the intercession of the saints, the recurring eruption of the "supernatural" in miracles—a vast continuity of beings between the seen and the unseen. Protestantism abolished most of these mediations. . . . It narrowed man's relationship to the sacred to the one exceedingly narrow channel that it called God's word.[4]

According to Berger, the tent poles of mystery, miracle, and magic were cut down. Only the tent pole of God's Word now held up the "sacred canopy" over the Western world.

For those of us in the Protestant tradition, this was a necessary correction, a return to biblical Christianity. But with the creation of more than one "version" of the Christian church came a questioning of religious tradition. As long as the tent pole of God's Word still stood, however, the tent did not collapse.

Then came the Enlightenment around 1700.[5] The Enlightenment was a kind of secular successor to the Reformation.[6] It split the world between the sciences and the humanities, between a kind of objective knowledge that is factual or scientific and therefore indisputable and our personal beliefs, opinions, values, and lifestyles, which are not indisputable.[7] The Enlightenment introduced the idea that we cannot talk about our beliefs and values as Truth but only as "your truth" and "my truth."

Augustine taught that "*unless* you believe, you will not understand." The Enlightenment reversed this, saying, "*If* you believe, you will not understand."[8] The Enlightenment claimed an objectivity that is not possible. John Locke, one of the early thinkers of the Enlightenment, said that "belief is no longer a higher power that reveals to us knowledge lying beyond the range of observation and reason, but merely a personal acceptance which falls short of empirical and rational demonstrability."[9] Belief was no longer in the service of knowledge but was an enemy that knowledge had to conquer.

What happens when we tear belief from knowledge? When we no longer need to believe that God reveals knowledge to us, we begin to exaggerate the part our own minds play in organizing knowledge. Immanuel Kant, following in Locke's footsteps suggested that knowledge, to be knowledge, must be certain, without the uncertainties of belief. There is no room for faith and no room for mystery. The mind must ensure that it is the master. Colin Gunton reminds us that too much light can blind us, and the "light" of the Enlightenment blinded many to their own prejudice against faith or belief.[10]

Then came the nineteenth century with the acceleration of scientific exploration in the wake of the Industrial Revolution. By the middle of the nineteenth century, Scottish Common Sense Realism had become the dominant philosophy in North America.[11] For Americans, it provided a firm foundation for a scientific approach to reality. Strict Calvinists had maintained that the human mind was blinded in humanity's fall from innocence. But in the Common Sense version, the intellect suffered from only a slight astigmatism.[12] Most evangelical Christians in the mid-nineteenth century believed that the Common Sense approach would provide a sure base for confirming rationally and scientifically the truths of the Bible and the Christian faith. "In an age that reverenced science, it was essential that this confidence in Scripture not be based on blind faith alone. God's truth was a unity, and so it was inevitable that science would confirm Scripture."[13]

But in 1869, Oliver Wendell Holmes predicted that the Bible would *not* stand up to scientific investigation. Just as the magnetic mountain had drawn all the nails and bolts from Sinbad's ship, so science would remove all credibility from the Bible. Evangelicals at that time pooh-poohed his prediction. When the Evangelical Alliance met in convention in 1873, European delegates warned American Christians of the danger of skepticism and rationalism, but American pastors were not alarmed. By then, Darwinism had begun its attack, hacking away at the tent pole of God's Word. But American theologians did not challenge the fundamental assumption of science—that truth can be reliably discovered by an objective examination of the facts that nature presents. Yet by the end of the nineteenth century, theology was no longer called the "queen of science." Religion had been split off as something "spiritual," having to do with the heart, not the head. Science could have its autonomy, and religion was beyond the reach of science. As aspects of Enlightenment philosophy have played out over the last three hundred years, even parts of the Christian church have lost the capacity to see God and to believe in the supernatural. Thus, the Enlightenment weakened the last pole holding up the sacred canopy of Christian belief in the Western world.

This is not to say that evangelical voices were silenced. A host of Christian leaders arose, crying in the wilderness. But the hold of Scripture on the wider society had been broken. Science could move forward without religious constraints. The Western world had been secularized. Note that none of this happened in *postmodern* times. It happened in *modern* times—the times in which people now over sixty years of age grew up.

Back in the mid-1980s, my husband and I spent a day at the Epcot Center in Orlando, Florida. At one exhibit a slogan in large letters reminded me that "if we can dream it, we can do it." In the last one hundred years, technology has shown us exactly that. We all benefit from much that technology has provided for us. I am writing this chapter on a computer with more power than I will ever use (while listening to the symphonies of Sibelius on the CD player by my desk). When I finish writing, I will go into the kitchen to cook dinner. I'll slice the carrots in the food processor, then nuke them in the microwave. I'll put salmon steaks on the smokeless electric grill and cook rice in the steamer. Am I happy with these tools in my office and my kitchen? Of course! I would not want to go back to writing books and cooking meals the way people did a hundred or even fifty years ago.

Coming out of the Enlightenment (which precipitated modern times), what is modern is always understood as intrinsically superior to everything that preceded it. Today's cars are better than cars made ten years ago or thirty years ago. We have nicer homes with bigger bathrooms and better appliances and roomier decks or patios. For us, the opposite of being modern is being backward, and who wants that? We like the fruits of modernity.

We may miss the fact, however, that modernity also brought relativism and pluralism into daily life, putting modernity on a collision course with Christian truth claims. Of course, religious belief and practice have not disappeared. But modernity has weakened the plausibility of Christian perceptions of reality for large numbers of people, mainly because the worldview of secularization has infiltrated the media and our school systems. Modernity is the social and intellectual culture that has shaped our Western civilization for the last three hundred years. It is our life-world and has provided the taken-for-granted assumptions we have about life.

In a perceptive critique of modernity, Peter Berger reminds us that modernity also brought us a sense of alienation from the deep human relationships we yearn for, an endless striving and restlessness with a mounting incapacity for repose, a mobility that leaves us unattached to concrete communities, a range of options that sometimes overwhelms us, and a secularization that deprives us of hope in the midst of suffering and evil.[14]

Much of what is blamed on postmodernism is not *post*modern at all. It is the direct consequence of "modern" thinking. Postmodernity, for all its faults, is an effort to correct some of the most disquieting evils of modernity. When hippies dropped out of American mainstream society in the 1960s and 1970s, many of them wanted to recapture the cohesive communities that they hoped would give them solidarity and meaning. They sought a less frantic lifestyle through "flower-power." And in their treks to ashrams in India or to TM mind-gurus in California, they hoped to find a sense of the transcendent. Many of those same hippies found the meaning they sought in the Jesus movement.

But we must live and work within a world in which many people do believe that "your truth isn't my truth" and "there is no such thing as 'true Truth.'" It was modernity that robbed theology of its truth-base by asserting that what could not be tested in a laboratory could not be verified. The postmoderns simply overturned the notion of objectivity in modern scientific assumptions. The certitudes based on an idea of objectivity were shown to be contaminated by the unconscious biases of the scientist conducting the research.

We must continue looking at epistemological shifts made by both men and women because these shifts take us to the heart of modern and postmodern thinking. The last two epistemological positions in both William Perry's and Mary Belenky's schemas are parallel for men and women, though they are not identical. Chapter 4 examined epistemological shifts some women make that are set in motion by their life experiences. Many women never shift from a passive way of knowing because their life experiences do not push them to do so. For other women, their life experiences shove them into a subjective-knower mode of thinking in which they refuse to accept as authoritative anything coming from an outside source unless it is corroborated by something in their own intuition.

Shifting to a Modern Way of Knowing

A different kind of life experience forces other women to make a shift to what Belenky called *procedural* knowledge. This is a distinctly modern way of knowing. In effect, this shift most often takes place when women go to school and are taught processes or procedures for analyzing things. Women learn formulas in algebra or geometry that allow them to move through a process to the right answer. In literature courses, they learn procedures for analyzing a poem or a play. Professors insist that there are proper ways or methods for thinking things through, and both men and women must learn them. In seminaries, they learn the process of exegesis in order to grasp the central idea of a biblical text, and they may also learn a process of hermeneutics for interpreting that text. Pastors teach their people processes for doing Bible study so that they do not move toward heresy as they read the Scriptures.

No longer is it enough to repeat verbatim what women have been taught by rote (as received knowers). Nor is it adequate to chatter on about intuitive feelings (as subjective knowers). In the academic world, women learn a process for doing systematic analysis. There are *procedures* for ferreting out truth, and as women learn them, they move to a different epistemology, a knowing what they know that comes because they follow procedures that lead to truth.

Both Perry and Belenky found that the next epistemological step for both men and women was to learn to "think like a modern."[15] We must learn to analyze and evaluate what is being taught. Not every college professor insists on this kind of critical thinking, of course, and people can graduate from college without having moved to this analytical epistemology in which we know what we know based on our ability to analyze and evaluate. But for those who have made this shift, the second functional question in preaching (Is it true?) becomes important in communication. The preacher who has procedural knowers in the congregation cannot settle for sermons exploring only the first functional question: What does the text mean? Those who have been taught to think critically often have serious faith questions that are never touched on or answered in church. A congregation made up of only passive knowers would not require preaching that explores the second functional question, but procedural knowers do need it.

Some women take to this analytical knowledge easily; others fight it as alien to their way of processing ideas. A great many women remain passive knowers all their lives, leaning exclusively on external authorities to give them answers. For those who make this epistemological shift, however, the rewards are great in the job market as well as in interpersonal relationships. Women who become analytical knowers experience an increasing sense of self-control in a world that becomes more manageable.[16] This kind of knowledge is "objective," a modern way of knowing. Women with this epistemology have a way of thinking and knowing that allows them to explore beyond what they have been told.[17]

According to Belenky, women often develop as "connected" analytical knowers. Instead of tearing into a book or a poem or an essay, they are more likely to ask, "What is this author saying to me?" This forms a connection between the person and the text. It is the development of intimacy with an idea. As one woman noted, "You shouldn't read a book just as something printed and distant from you, but as a real experience of someone who went through some sort of situation."[18] When a connected procedural knower asks, "Why do you think that?" she doesn't mean, "What were the steps in your reasoning?" Rather, she is asking, "What circumstances in your life led you to that perception?" Connected analytical knowers, according to Belenky, start with an interest in the facts of other people's lives but gradually shift their focus to other people's ways of thinking.

Analytical knowers are objective in the sense that they focus on something to be analyzed or understood. Women who rely on this way of knowing are systematic thinkers, but their thinking is confined within the systems or processes of analysis they have learned. Belenky states that a procedural knower can be a liberal or a conservative but cannot be a radical because the system controls what can or cannot be known.[19] But some procedural knowers yearn for a personal way of knowing that goes beyond the systems they have been taught or the relationships and institutions in which they have worked. They begin to move out of procedural knowing.

Shifting Again to a More Postmodern Way of Knowing

As some women move to the fifth epistemological position,[20] it appears that they are concerned about weaving together strands of both rational and emotional thought, integrating objective and subjective knowing. Women with this epistemology (called *constructed knowledge* by Belenky) have a desire to be free from the standards and reasons of others, but not in the same manner as subjective knowers. Whereas subjective knowers have a passion for knowing the self, and analytical knowers are excited about the power of reason, women with an epistemology of constructed knowing borrow from different ways of knowing to weave together a new way of knowing.

These knowers no longer dutifully come up with answers when questions are asked. Instead, they ask *who* is asking the question, *why* the question is being asked, and *how* answers are arrived at. Often they conclude that the question is the wrong question to ask or that it is out of context. This has implications for how they may evaluate sermons they hear.

When women take responsibility for evaluating their assumptions about knowledge, doing so changes the respect they once gave to experts. They appreciate expertise but back away from calling anyone an expert. For them, true experts must reveal an appreciation for complexity and must show humility about their knowledge. The theories and recommendations of experts must be grounded in real life and the data of the everyday. Experts have to show that they "listen" to people and give equal weight to experience and abstractions. Because a pastor is seen as an "expert" on God, women with this way of knowing bring the same expectations to church.

Posing questions is central to their way of knowing. Such women resolve moral conflicts not by calling up a logical hierarchy of abstract principles but through trying to understand the conflict in the context of each person's perspective, needs, and goals—and then doing the best possible for each one involved.

More than any other group, these women are seriously occupied with the moral or spiritual dimension of their lives.[21] They insist that every choice be made by considering the effects it will have on others. Their vision is of a full and complex life rather than of a single commitment. These women mix idealism and realism. They want to make a difference in the world, but at the same time, they recognize their limitations.

How Does This Apply to Preaching?

This last way of knowing has much in common with the question-posing and acceptance of ambiguity in postmodernism. Yet it is not completely postmodern. These women have not discarded linear ways of thinking, but they have insisted on doing analysis as it is embedded in a life in the community. While sermons to analytical knowers should deal with the second functional question, demanding proof and argument, for this final group of women, it is the third functional question that matters: So what? But the so-what answer cannot be canned or pat. It must deal with the consequences of the biblical text for people where they live.

These women know that something is profoundly wrong with our culture, and many of them seek a spirituality that will help them make sense of it all. (Chapter 6 examines issues of faith and spirituality for women.) We do not minister effectively to them unless we ourselves have wrestled with questions of pain and suffering in our world. These women are not looking for pat answers, nor are they looking merely for explanations. They ask their questions in the context of people's real pain, understanding that every human situation is complex.

As we review Perry's and Belenky's research, we are reminded once again that differences *within* groups are often much greater than differences *between* groups. While researchers report some differences between male and female knowers, the gap is not so much between men and women as it is between women who do not know that they can know anything, women who know only what they have received from an external authority, women who reject all external authorities, women who learn to acquire knowledge through analysis, and women who construct a way of knowing by combining both external and internal resources. That is the spread a preacher may face from the pulpit each week.

Every sermon probably cannot reach every person every time. For some listeners, it is enough that you deal with the first functional question: What does the text mean? For others, that is inadequate. They need proof that what the text says is true for them (the second functional question). For still others, a relevant sermon must answer the third functional question: So what? What difference does this biblical text make in the lives of hurting men and women in my neighborhood or in my family?

Some congregations are made up primarily of passive knowers. Other churches appeal to a broader range of knowers.[22] Part of your audience analysis is to understand what kind of knowers fill your pews. How do you come to such an understanding? Listening to what people say about your sermon at the conclusion of a service will give you some clues about what they are hearing and how they are processing it. If you attend to this long enough, you will begin to form a fairly good assessment of the range of epistemologies into which you speak each week.

Understanding how people in the pews know what they know can be helpful, but it is certainly not the entire story. God's Word has the power to break into any way of knowing, and God's Spirit enables listeners to hear that life-changing Word. At the same time, attention to all three functional questions over the course of your preaching can make it easier for every listener to hear God's voice more clearly. In the process, you will speak God's truth in ways that both modern and postmodern listeners can hear.

One thing has become abundantly clear to me in recent years: Many women hunger for the Word of God made accessible in a manner that speaks to their situations. Whenever I speak at women's conferences or retreats, I sense a profound hunger for help that is grounded in biblical truth. Many ministries to women suffer from acute shallowness, but I also hear women complain that the Word spoken from the pulpit is also shallow. If we are to be faithful to our calling, we must do more than merely buttress secular insights with some verses from the Bible. We must build strong biblical foundations so that women (and men) have the tools to deal with daily life. This means that when we open the Word of God to any audience, we must work from the text. We meet the needs of all knowers by solid exegesis, not by a casual or passing reference to a Bible verse—or even by piling up half a dozen verses from different parts of the Bible. We must wrestle with the implications of the text within its context, dealing with the "is it true" question for our listeners with primarily analytical epistemologies. And we must apply texts carefully to people's lives, not in a one-size-fits-all manner but with an awareness of the uniqueness of everyone's life situations. Only then will we begin to feed women's hunger with real substance.

Recently, I spoke at a women's retreat on the West Coast. The audience was made up mostly of women under forty or forty-five, and the majority came for a fun weekend. Though many of them were from an evangelical church, few brought Bibles. They attended the retreat not because they wanted to listen to a speaker but because they wanted to kick back and enjoy a time-out from daily life. (Much of the retreat planning had focused on assuring the women of a relaxing weekend.) In the first evening session, I began with a relevant hypothetical situation about driving to a grocery store, a story that brought laughter and set the stage for the thrust of the four Bible studies I would give over the weekend on making choice choices in life. I then immediately moved to the biblical text and stayed there, walking through the narrative (first functional question), raising legitimate questions about the activities of the principals (second functional question), and moving toward the application of the central idea of the text (third functional question). In the second and third sessions, I did not spend any time setting up a "funny" contemporary introduction but immediately moved the listeners into the chosen texts, dealing again with all three functional questions. On Sunday morning I again started from life in today's world, then moved into the biblical texts. While the overarching topic for the weekend was "Making Choice Choices," each session was an in-depth Bible study that kept the women focused on God's revelation of truth before moving to its application to their lives in today's world. Despite fairly widespread indifference in the beginning to the idea of listening to a Bible teacher four times throughout the weekend, woman after woman came to thank me for teaching them the Scriptures in a way that met their needs. Many of them had not come primarily to be fed God's Word, but when it happened, they knew God had met them, and their lives were being changed.

There is a famine in our land for the Word of the Lord. The audience is complex. But God somehow reaches a diverse group of people with life-changing truth when we give attention to all three functional questions, speaking God's Word to modern and postmodern listeners.

Summing Up the Chapter

- Often our messages are fuzzy because we ourselves are so embedded in our culture that we cannot discern the difference between what lasts and what passes away.
- Postmodernism scares many Christians because we connect it to the absence of values and truth in American society today.
- It was modernity (not postmodernity) that brought relativism and pluralism into daily life, putting modernity on a collision course with Christian truth claims by stating that what could not be tested in a laboratory could not be verified as truth.
- Modernity has brought us a sense of alienation from the deep human relationships we yearn for, an endless striving and restlessness with a mounting incapacity for repose, a mobility that leaves us unattached to concrete communities, a range of options that sometimes overwhelms us, and a secularization that deprives us of hope in the midst of suffering and evil.

- Analytical knowers are objective systematic thinkers who focus on something to be analyzed or understood.
- Constructed knowers do not merely come up with answers to questions others ask but delve deeper: Who is asking the question? Why is the question being asked? How are answers arrived at? Often they conclude that the question being asked is not a valid question. This has implications for how they evaluate sermons they hear.
- Part of audience analysis is to discover what kinds of knowers fill your pews. You can get a sense of the range of epistemologies in your congregation by listening to people's comments at the end of a service, noting what they heard and how they processed it.
- The Holy Spirit enables listeners to hear the life-changing Word, but your preaching can make it easier for every listener to hear God's voice more clearly.

Questions to Ponder

- Reflecting on your own enculturation, how do you see yourself in the light of modern and postmodern philosophies and questions about life? How does that influence your preaching?
- With what kind of audience are you most comfortable? Do you prefer preaching to passive listeners or to people who often raise disconcerting questions?
- How comfortable are you with preaching sermons based on or including the second functional question (Is it true?)?
- How comfortable are you with preaching sermons based on or including the third functional question (So what?)?
- What is the relevance of an analytical approach in a world increasingly focused on relationships?

6

Women, Spirituality, and Issues of Faith

Over the years I have known many women whose hearts have echoed Amy Carmichael's prayer:

> From prayer that asks that I may be
> Sheltered from winds that beat on Thee;
> From fearing when I should aspire,
> From faltering when I should climb higher,
> From silken self, O Captain, free
> Thy soldier who would follow Thee.
>
> From subtle love of softening things,
> From easy choices, weakenings, . . .
> From all that dims Thy Calvary,
> O Lamb of God, deliver me.

Some women who prayed that prayer found their way to remote parts of the world, desiring only that God would

> Give me the love that leads the way,
> The faith that nothing can dismay
> The hope no disappointments tire

The passion that will burn like fire,
Let me not sink to be a clod:
Make me Thy fuel, Flame of God.[1]

Yet whether at home or in a distant mission, while some women realized the results of that prayer in their lives and their work, others more often found little that challenged them to this level of commitment in daily life and activity. Churches and mission-sending agencies frequently reduced their usefulness and confined their commitment to trivial pursuits so that whatever vision had set their feet on the high road of tireless, loving service for Jesus Christ was dimmed, even extinguished.[2] I have known and wept for these women.

Other women who at some point prayed Carmichael's prayer succumbed to "the subtle love of softening things" available in our culture and often valued more highly in our churches than the quirkiness of "leaving all" to follow Jesus. In such cases, service to God was reduced to ever more trivial pursuits that made earlier commitments to Christ seem not only unrealistic but also ridiculous.[3]

Still others began as lovers of God only to feel that the Christian church had no place for them, and eventually the flame of biblical faith within them died. Carol Christ, an Old Testament scholar and at one time a devout Christian, wrote these haunting words:

> While women sit silent, perhaps even unaware that they are deadening themselves in order to do so, others leave the churches and synagogues, cutting off their relation with the biblical God. In both cases, women who once had powerful feelings about the God of biblical tradition may be denying part of themselves. They may be deadening their religious sensibility altogether, suppressing powerful, conflicting feelings toward God that come to them, perhaps, "in the night, tinged with hatred, with remorse, but most of all with infinite yearning."[4] A woman who swallows her anger and bitterness at God may also cut off her longing for the God who provoked her to anger.[5]

In the same book, *Laughter of Aphrodite: Reflections on a Journey to the Goddess,* Carol Christ details the reasons for her decision to leave historic Christianity and become a "priestess of Aphrodite."[6] A blurb on the book jacket quotes theologian Elizabeth Schüssler-Fiorenza, who noted that "Christians of all persuasions need to heed her passionate challenge to how we conceive and speak of God."

How do you "conceive and speak of God"? And how does that affect women in the church? How can pastors encourage a spiritual formation in women that is anchored in Scripture and becomes a permanent habit of the heart, soul, and mind? How is the preaching task essential to that spiritual formation?

The question of women's spirituality (how they know and relate to God) cannot be separated from epistemology (how we know what we know). Spirituality, most simply put, has to do with knowing God. (One writer describes it as learning to hear and respond to the call of God in our lives.[7] Joann Wolski Conn speaks of Christian spirituality as a self-transcending experience of God, through Christ, by the gift of the Holy Spirit: "Christian spirituality includes every dimension of human life.")[8] But the "knowing" is not an abstract knowledge of a doctrine of God; it is a personal relationship with the personal God. It is the difference between the French verb *savoir,* meaning knowing a fact, and *connaitre,* meaning knowing a person. Spirituality is not less than cognitive, but it is more than cognitive. It is growth in a relationship with the living God.

It is not difficult to see how various epistemologies can block women from entering fully into that relationship, responding to the call of God. The following pages explore some of the difficulties women with different epistemologies may encounter as they try to love God with their whole mind. Many women are seriously occupied with the moral and spiritual dimensions of their lives. In that sense, they are wide open to God. At the same time, they may ask questions that go unanswered from the pulpit or are answered in ways that do not ring true to their experience or to their understanding of Scripture. These women may look elsewhere for answers and hope.

To talk about spirituality for women is complicated because each of the five epistemologies discussed in chapters 4 and 5 has different implications for spirituality. If you preach, you may want to take a moment to consider your congregation on any given Sunday morning, thinking about the women who listen to you each week. Can you discern where they may be in terms of their way of knowing what they know? If so, you can begin to think about the ways in which you need to speak of God in order to reach these women.

To unpack the issue of women's spiritualities and their connection to preaching, this chapter will first revisit the five epistemologies examined in chapters 4 and 5, looking particularly at the barriers to loving God with whole minds present in each. Then the chapter will explore the task of preaching so that women in each of these categories can come to know God's voice and respond biblically to his call in their lives.

Spirituality for Women Who Live in Silence

Do you know any women in your congregation who live in silence? These are the women who experience themselves as mindless and voiceless, who do not know that they know anything. One woman named Ann, looking back to the time when she lived in silence, described it this way:

> I could never understand what they were talking about. My schooling was very limited. I didn't learn anything. I would just sit there and let people ramble on about something I didn't understand and would say, "Yup, yup." I would be too embarrassed to ask, "What do you really mean?"[9]

Even though women who live in silence often have the gifts of intelligence and their five senses, they are unaware that they have such gifts.

This does not mean that such women cannot survive in the world. Ann supported her family financially and reared the children. Her husband's drinking, violence, and theft of the family's meager resources kept her busy ensuring the survival of her children and herself. But because, in her words, "I was brought up thinking a woman was supposed to be very feminine and sit back and let the man do all the stuff,"[10] Ann saw her husband as the source of her security, thinking that only he could figure things out.

Mary Belenky and her colleagues found that such women usually grew up in isolation, with few friends and without much play or dialogue. Their families were not part of the wider community.[11] Lev Vygotsky noted that people who do not talk out loud with other people cannot talk through things inside their own minds. A woman living in silence does not "carry on a conversation" with herself. Without playing, talking, and listening to others, people do not develop a sense that they can think things through.[12]

Knowing God, for women who live in silence, will likely come only through the patient love and modeling of other women who know God. Because silent women have not discovered their capacity for thinking, preaching has little effect on them. While they will try to obey any commands that are preached (because to fail to do so could bring disaster on them), the obedience they give will not likely be a loving response to the God with whom they have a relationship. Women with this epistemology have few resources for understanding the gospel apart from seeing it lived out by women close to them whom they trust.

Spirituality for Received Knowers

Of all the men and women sitting in church on Sunday morning, the passive knowers are possibly the most "desirable" as listeners. Listening is their way of knowing. In contrast to women who live in silence, these listeners rely on words as *central* to knowing. They are open to taking in what others, especially those in authority, have to offer. At the same time, they have little confidence in their own ability to speak unless they can repeat what they have received from an expert of some sort. As noted in chapter 4, received knowers do not believe they can generate knowledge through reflection on their own experiences. They gather facts but seldom develop their own opinions.

Because passive knowers think that every question has only one right answer, they cannot deal with paradox. Several contradictory ideas can never match up with the facts of a case at the same time. When asked, "What if your experts disagreed?" one woman resolved this unimaginable dilemma by saying, "I'd just have to go with what most people believe in."[13]

Belenky and her colleagues noted that passive knowers have trouble with poetry, wondering why poets do not simply come out and say what they really mean. For them, every poem has only one interpretation.[14] Passive knowers are literal. They read the lines and follow the plot, but they cannot read between the lines because they do not believe there *is* anything between the lines. They think that people who read between the lines are making things up. They want clarity.[15]

When passive knowers listen, they often take many notes, storing first in their notebooks and later in their heads a kind of photocopy of the sermon. They do not ask the second or third functional question; they merely file the information "as is." Such knowers are confident about their ability to absorb and store the truth received from others. They may even see themselves as richly endowed repositories of that information, and they are usually successful students whenever they do not have to engage in personal reflection. In many cases, they can reproduce received information when asked to speak or teach, but they may feel threatened if asked to apply it or to produce their own study.

The language of received knowers is sprinkled generously with words such as *should, ought,* or *must* when trying to solve a moral problem. As noted in chapter 4, they work hard to do what others tell them is good or right. While the *shoulds, oughts,* and *musts* are the comfortable ground of decision-making for such women, these words often generate the wrong kind of guilt. And because these women cannot tolerate ambiguity, there is never a situation in which what is right (a *should* or a *must*) for one woman is not also right for every other woman. Everything is either-or. The spirituality of such women is externally directed and often carries an implicit judgmental stance toward others.[16]

Some teaching in the Bible can be confusing to passive knowers because it permits certain actions in some cases and not in others. For example, when the apostle Paul discusses whether first-century Gentile Christians should purchase meat in the marketplace that had previously been offered to a pagan idol (1 Corinthians 8), he states that while "an idol is nothing" and Christians can eat such meat, they should refrain from doing so if their actions would cause a weaker Christian to fall away from the faith. Many passive knowers find this case-by-case approach to moral decision-making perplexing.

A passive knower is looking for correct doctrine, a clear unambiguous statement of faith that anchors her in the Christian life. She sits in the pew week after week, waiting for the truths that confirm her in "the faith," the theological or doctrinal basis of the Christian life. These women thrive on Bible study that "goes deep" in exegesis. They prefer preaching that marshals facts neatly with no loopholes or ambiguities.

Carol Gilligan found that passive knowers (believing that women should be listeners, subordinate and unassertive) think that if they excel, those they love will suffer for it.[17] Women who have been taught that passivity is the proper and godly role for Christian women may well neglect to use the gifts of God within them for ministry, somehow believing that doing so would put others at risk.

The capacity for spirituality in received knowers is limited by their inability to process the truth they take in. They have the ability to absorb many facts, but they are incapable of evaluating those facts. Thus, their spirituality expands only to the degree that the spiritual authorities in their lives give them sound guidance. A received knower sitting under the preaching of a deeply spiritual guide may develop a strong relationship with God, but her inability to process what she is taught may keep her from loving God with her whole mind.

Spirituality for Subjective Knowers

The shift to subjective knowing is significant for women when and if it occurs. These formerly passive women begin to pay attention to a small voice inside their own heads, and they come to value it. They develop a growing awareness of an *inner* power to think that transforms the way they know what they know.

Many (though not all) subjective knowers had a parent or spouse who belittled them or squelched their curiosity or chastised them for asking questions. As a result, they spent their lives looking for a faithful authority to whom they could attach themselves. But what researchers found most consistently was a failed authority figure in their lives. These knowers had put their trust in esteemed teachers, religious spokesmen, or respected professionals who, in one way or another, had let them down. For many women who moved to subjective knowing, their sense of disappointment and outrage about this occurrence was pervasive.[18]

Chapter 4 detailed this shift from passive to subjective knowing. When women begin this shift, they tend to listen less to public authorities (e.g., pastors, teachers, politicians) and turn to people closer to their own experience—female peers, mothers, sisters, and grandmothers. Truth, for these transitional women, is found in the firsthand experience of others most like themselves. The discovery that firsthand experience is a valuable source of knowledge gives daily life new meaning. A woman of forty-eight, returning to school to develop skills necessary to support her children, described the moment she knew something had to change:

> I always thought there were rules and that if you followed the rules, you'd be happy. And I never understood why I wasn't [happy]. I'd get to thinking, gee, I'm good, I follow the rules. I do everything they tell me to, and things don't go right for me. My life was a mess. I wrote to a priest that I was very fond of and I asked him, "What do I do to make things right?" He had no answers. This time it dawned on me that I was not going to get the answers from anybody. I would have to find them myself.[19]

Subjective knowing can take different forms. Some subjective knowers become polite listeners, spectators on the sideline, watching and listening but not acting. The loneliness of these hidden reticent women is striking as they stand in sharp contrast to the confident passive knowers in their circle. They may come to believe that the outward conformity of passive knowers is a lie and does not reveal the inner truth or potential they have recently come to value in themselves. Other subjective knowers nurture a strong trust in their own subjective truth, feeling at times a personal omnipotence over all external authorities. They want to live a carefree and unrestrained life. One woman described herself in these words: "I've never had a personality. I've always been someone's daughter, someone's wife, someone's mother. Right now I'm so busy being born, discovering who I am, that I don't know who I am. And I don't know where I'm going. And everything is going to be fine!"[20] All subjective knowers come to the point of disregarding the knowledge and advice of experts. Authority no longer comes from somewhere outside themselves but from within their own minds.

Truth for a subjective knower comes through her personal intuition, not from outside teachers (or from more complex epistemologies). Because this new truth is intuited, not learned, she sees herself as a mysterious conduit for truth, not as a processor of truth. Truth is no longer something she receives from outside herself. It develops inside her. How then does a subjective knower know truth? She *feels* satisfied or comfortable when "truth" has emerged. Faith, if it exists for her, is her intuition about God and her willingness to trust that intuition and go wherever it takes her. It is in that intuition or feeling that she "hears" God's voice. Preaching to help such a woman love God with her whole *mind* may be ineffective until she has come to love God with her whole *soul*.

Some social scientists have speculated that these women arrive at this point because of an ingrained belief that men think and women feel, and thus a woman should not try to think because it interferes with her ability to feel.[21] Ideas come from men and may or may not have any real relevance for women's lives.[22]

Contrary to the passive knower, who is eager for "the truth," subjective knowers tend to tune out the preaching or teaching of men, attending only to the insights of women close to them. When a subjective knower is faced with advice from external experts that contradicts her own experience and inner voice, she often responds pragmatically, "I do what works best for me." It is common for subjective knowers to insist that everyone's experience is unique and therefore no one has the right to speak for others or to judge what others have to say. As one subjective knower put it, "You have to be in a situation to know what is right or wrong. You can't look at someone from a distance and say, 'Well, they should do this or that.' Maybe it wouldn't work for everybody."[23] Another expressed it this way: "Anyone's interpretation is valid if that's the way they see it. . . . I mean nobody can tell you that your opinion is wrong, you know."[24] This stance effectively wards off much of the teaching contained in sermons.

Subjective knowers appear to distrust logic, analysis, abstraction, and even language itself. Often when these women speak, they argue against those who, in society, hold the keys to truth—doctors, teachers, scientists, and others. It is as if they have to deny any strategies for knowing that they think belong to the authorities in their world. This sometimes results in a distrust of books in favor of learning through direct experience. The bottom line for these women is that truth is personal and private.

The danger to spirituality for a subjective knower is obvious: If she accepts as true only those things she can intuit and she rejects all teaching from authorities, she cuts herself off from most of what nourishes spiritual life. Her insistence on her own truth leaves her vulnerable to heresy of many sorts, and the possibility of learning to love God with her whole mind is short-circuited because she is not open to truth from any source except her own experience.

Spirituality for Procedural Knowers

The epistemological shift to procedural knowledge is a shift to the voice of reason. As detailed in chapter 5, this most often takes place when women in school are taught procedures that lead to knowing by analysis. While some schools allow (even encourage) students to go no further than repeating verbatim what the professors have said in lectures, other schools insist that students learn processes for doing systematic or critical analysis. There are procedures for discovering truth, and students must base what they know on the right use of the procedures that lead to truth.

Procedural knowledge is a modern "objective" way of knowing: It relies on logic, analysis, and evaluation because truth is not something you just know. Knowledge is not always immediately accessible, but procedures or processes allow a person to explore beyond what he or she has been told by an expert. In effect, these procedures hand the tools of linear thinking to the person willing to learn to use them. The emphasis is always on procedures, skills, and techniques.[25]

Many women who are procedural knowers refuse to judge others according to an impersonal standard but instead try to understand the other person's reasons or actions. They seem to take naturally to a non-judgmental stance. Even when they disagree strongly with an opinion, they hesitate to judge it wrong until they have tried to understand the reasoning behind it. For this reason, biblical preaching that appears to judge the behavior or attitude of someone on the basis of an abstract principle may be rejected unless the preacher describes a process of trying to get inside the offender's mind and heart.

It is easy to condemn this refusal to judge as being soft on sin. Yet in procedural knowers' minds, this is not the case. They separate the sin from the sinner. All of us know of situations in which a person was judged unfairly, a judgment that remained long after the person was cleared. Procedural knowers would argue for a careful investigation and analysis before any judgment is passed.

Faith for these procedural knowers means having confidence in the God who personally cares for them and who reveals truth to them. Faith is intimately tied to their vision or image of God. They want to have a personal relationship with *God,* not with a theological abstraction.

Knowing God and responding to his call on their lives (the essence of spirituality) are not difficult for procedural knowers if they have been given a biblical vision of God.

Spirituality for Constructed Knowers

The procedural knower's sense of self is identified with methods or procedures.[26] But some women look for a way to construct knowledge that allows them to combine both the inner voice and the procedural knower's methods of logical analysis. They do not want to abandon the tools of analysis, but they do not want to be confined to them either. Academic settings often insist that learners "weed out the self," the subjective inner voice, from analysis. Some women want to integrate that inner voice with outer skills. They want to weave their passions and their intellectual life into a single cloth. In a sense, these women want to get acquainted with the self within them. They do this by asking themselves many questions about themselves: Who am I? What should my life be about? Christian women at this point also ask, What responsibilities do I have to myself and to others? What responsibilities do I have to God and to the family of God? How am I to live my life? As noted in chapter 5, constructed knowers, more than any other knowers, are seriously occupied with the moral and spiritual dimensions of their lives.

These women are also passionate knowers. Samuel Huntington identified four different responses people give to stress in their lives (see chap. 4). Of the four types of responders, those who develop what he called moral passion are those who most deeply desire satisfying answers to their questions, closing any gap between their ideal and their reality. The woman who develops moral passion, however, risks the most. A woman who has pursued faith with passion but does not find the answers she needs or the resolution she seeks will begin to question the institutions and authority of those giving what to her are unacceptable answers. At some point, if satisfying answers are not forthcoming, she leaves the institutions that have failed her. In this sense, she resembles the subjective knower. Her leaving, however, is not driven merely by subjective feelings but also by rationality. The result, however, is the same. She leaves.

These women also have a capacity for "attentive love,"[27] the ability to imagine and be sensitive to the inner life of others to the point that it becomes a moral commitment. These women not only *think* about their moral and spiritual lives but also try to translate their moral commitments into action, believing that they have a responsibility to the larger community in which they live.[28] But for these women, shaping and acting on their commitments is not a clear-cut linear movement from here to there. It becomes a juggling act as they try to balance their commitments to children's schedules, spouses, the needs of friends and parents, and their own personal nurture in reading and learning. In the case of Christian women, they must also balance their walk with God. These are not driven super-women, trying to do it all. They are ordinary women who see the necessity of serving others while still finding a means to attend to their own spiritual and intellectual growth.

Constructed knowers have the epistemological tools for a deep spirituality. Their desire to weave together their inner voice and their intellectual life, their moral passion and their capacity for attentive love provides a strong fabric for constructing a deep and lasting relationship with God.

How Does This Apply to Preaching?

As cited earlier in this chapter, Joann Wolski Conn defines Christian spirituality as a self-transcending experience of God, through Christ, by the gift of the Holy Spirit.[29] We cannot transcend ourselves and experience God except by faith. Preaching is in one way or another a call to faith. But what do we mean by "faith"? The writer to the Hebrew Christians described faith as "the substance of things hoped for, the evidence of things not seen" (Heb. 11:1). For some women, such a definition of faith is a stumbling block: How can one know for sure something that cannot be objectively verified, that one is called to believe without seeing? For others, faith is a no-brainer: It simply means trusting God. For still others, faith is "the faith," the historic Christian faith, the creed recited in church each week. It is what one believes to be true about God, humanity, and God's work in the world.

Faith can pose problems for the parishioners who listen to your sermons each week. Some wrestle with the difference between *knowing* and *believing*. Others struggle with the fact of many different ideas about God, wondering which one is correct. Still others wonder merely how much faith is enough faith to get them to heaven. Some find faith difficult, even impossible, in the face of their life experiences. For example, women who were sexually violated by a father find it difficult to trust anyone, especially someone whom they have been taught to call "Father." Their trust in God seemed misplaced when bad things happened to them in the innocence of childhood.

If there is any subject in the Bible about which preachers must not be vague or abstract, it is the subject of faith. For the biblical writers, faith is not a theoretical question. It met them and it meets us in the middle of life in the world. Faith is the door to the presence of God (Heb. 11:6). Faith is the means by which we appropriate God's grace for salvation (Eph. 2:8–9). Faith is the root of the Christian life (Rom. 5:1). Faith unleashes power to serve God (Matt. 17:20). In short, faith is at the core of the Christian life. Preaching is a call to faith, and it must be clear. Without faith we cannot please God (Heb. 11:6). Without faith a relationship with God is not possible. Faith is essential to Christian spirituality.

Yet women who know what they know in different ways will likely come at faith in different ways. The barriers they must overcome are often fashioned from beliefs that have little to do with biblical truth.

How can preachers preach to the various epistemologies of women in order to bring all women to faith and a deeper spirituality?

For silent women, church programs that bring them together with small groups of women for informal fellowship can be a means of helping them begin the journey to another way of knowing themselves and their world and thus to understanding what they hear in sermons. It may be in the testimony of another woman that a silent woman begins to "know" that God in heaven loves her with an infinite love. As she hears other women pray she may learn about the possibility of having her own personal conversation with God. The key to unlocking the minds of women who live in silence may be nothing more than frequent contact and conversation with women who love God with their minds and talk about his empowering presence in their lives.

Without this shift, the spirituality of such women is stunted because their minds cannot absorb the abstractions of much Christian teaching. Church-based programs for women can be a door to a new epistemology for these women; even more, such programs can be the door to a new life in Jesus Christ for them. Any program in the church that brings women of any age together just to talk has the potential for helping women who live in silence. These women learn best from other women who live out their faith in a loving God in daily life.

Passive knowers, as noted in chapter 4, seek out the most qualified expert they can find, usually someone others have praised as "the best in the field." If you are the acknowledged "expert" preacher, then you will have the undivided attention of such women. But if you appear to be unsure of something, this can raise questions about your expertise. Such women do not tolerate ambiguity. It is all or nothing with them. If it is right, it is totally right; if it is only partly right, it is worthless.

The preaching that connects for them is the sermon built around the first functional question: What does the text mean? Preaching that works from the second functional question (Is it true?) or the third (So what?) may strike passive knowers as irrelevant and even unsettling. A preacher must preach the whole counsel of God and cannot avoid the second and third functional questions. At the same time, it is important to delve into the biblical text (first functional question) so that passive listeners can take something solid away from the sermon.

A positive/negative theme in the moral thought of passive knowers is the call to care for and empower others while remaining selfless. One of the great gifts of many women to humanity is their ability and desire to reach out to and care for others.[30] The church would be impoverished without this ongoing gift given freely by myriads of women. But one of the great deceptions of self-giving is the notion that it is necessary to annihilate the self in order to help others. There is no self to give if there is no self. Some teachings on biblical humility and self-surrender to God focus on self-effacement. Women imbued with this come to believe that acting on their own behalf to develop and use their natural and spiritual gifts is a sign of pride or a failure to submit to God's will. Such women may need to be told that the sin lies not in taking action to develop their God-given gifts but in failing to value the gifts God has given them enough to develop and use them. Just as the Proverbs 31 woman "girds herself with strength, and strengthens her arms" (v. 17) for her work, women today need to hear that it is good and right for them to pursue whatever education and experience they need to be all that God has gifted them to be.

Because subjective knowers have closed their minds to teaching by external authority figures, sermons work best when they reach into narrative biblical literature. A pastor does well to use the stories of biblical *women's* direct experiences of God—God's provision, God's help, God's instruction—as a means of bringing biblical truth to these women. It should go without saying, but any presentation of biblical women's lives should be done in a positive way. Cheap shots at women's apparent foibles may draw smiles or laughter from some men in the congregation, but they will draw only polite silence from most women.[31] If there is to be any penetration of the gospel into the minds of subjective knowers or any development of a relationship with God, they will come through the modeling of faith and spirituality by biblical and contemporary women.

Procedural knowers want to have a personal relationship with *God,* not with a theological abstraction. Faith for such women means having confidence in the God who personally cares and who reveals truth to them. As a result, faith is intimately tied to their vision or image of God. For such knowers, effective preaching focuses on who God is and how God relates to them.

In 1953, J. B. Phillips wrote a small but powerful book titled *Your God Is Too Small.*[32] In it he introduced readers to inadequate visions or images of God that many Christians hold—God as a resident policeman, or as a parental hangover, or as a grand old man, or as a heavenly bosom, among others. The kind of preaching to which laypeople are exposed in large measure determines the vision or image of God they carry around in their heads, and that vision determines how they live. If they see God as an arbitrary dictator or as a spoilsport, they live in fear or guilt. Their vision of God is central to their lives because that vision provides the world-view that controls them. It shapes the way they both interpret and respond to everything going on around them.

The call to faith for procedural knowers must be a call to a God-sized God, perhaps pieced together from the kaleidoscope of images the Bible provides to help us know God: God as Creator of all that is (Gen. 1:1; John 1:3), God as an approachable Father (Matt. 6:8–9), God as the sovereign King "high and lifted up" (Isa. 6:1), God as the good and faithful shepherd (Psalm 23), God as an eagle bearing us up (Exod. 19:4; Deut. 32:10–14), God as a mother nourishing and comforting us (Isa. 66:12–13), God as our rock and fortress protecting and hiding us in time of trouble (Ps. 31:1–3). All of these are ways of visualizing God, of forming pictures in our minds that help us grasp some part of who God is. Only as these great varied visions of God are held up to procedural knowers week after week will they learn to exercise faith.

The preacher needs a sanctified imagination to convey a worthy vision of God, painting pictures on women's minds of the all-powerful, all-wise, and trustworthy God whose love never ceases. This spectrum of images of God tells us that no single image of God is enough for a rich, adequate, strong faith in diverse life situations. We cannot reduce this wide range of images to a single doctrine. In times of devastation, women need to know that the Creator God is committed to bringing something good and new out of death and disorder (Isa. 43:2–3; Rev. 21:5). In times of acute physical need, women need to know the Shepherd God who guides the sheep into green pastures (Psalm 23). In times of deep spiritual need, they need to know the Redeemer God who blots out iniquities and remembers our sins no more (Ps. 103:1–12). Preaching to procedural knowers means preaching a vision of God adequate to every circumstance in life. It is that vision of God that enables women to love him with all their minds as well as with their hearts and souls.

Preaching to constructed knowers is best done in humility, showing an appreciation for the complexity of human life in a sinful world and promising no more (but no less) than Scripture promises as the means for coping with that complexity as a lover and follower of Jesus Christ.

What are the spiritual needs of constructed knowers? One need is for balance in their lives. A church with ubiquitous needs for volunteer workers can pile many responsibilities on such women because they want, above all, to help others. But that can work against such women's own need for time with God and the Bible. It can work against their responsibilities to their families and neighbors. And it can work against their own personal growth, denying them time to read and grow. Furthermore, many tasks are passed off to women in the church without thought given to a match between gift and task. A constructed knower may take on a task that needs to be done just because no one else will do it. But if she sees no change in people's lives because of her work, it will become counterproductive for her. Her mind and heart must be engaged in helping others find a new life and a better life, one in which she and those she serves can thrive.

Faith for these women must include a broad vision of God. The vision they have of God shapes not only how they trust or distrust God but also their moral decision-making. W. Edward Everding Jr. and Dana W. Wilbanks put it this way:

> Faith is central to our decision making since we make decisions on the basis of whom we trust or what we care about most. The object of our trusting and caring functions as the center of our lives or the god of our lives. . . . For the decision maker, the Bible's core and disturbing questions are: "Who is your God?" "Whom will you serve?"[33]

Because these women are actively engaged in helping others (as a moral commitment), they constantly make decisions about how to use their time. Only the vision of a God-sized God will be adequate to their decision-making needs. Like the Proverbs 31 woman, they want to give themselves to what lasts, not to what passes away (v. 30). Their lives must be grounded in "the fear of the Lord," that is, the knowledge of the eternal God as Creator, Redeemer, and Sustainer of their lives. As Stuart Olyott stated:

> The fear of God is a habit of mind which acknowledges him at every step, and which views everything in relation to him who is eternally holy, just and good. It is not the degrading and demoralizing dread of his power such as can be found in many pagan religions, but an inward attitude which loves him, is aware that life is lived in his presence and which longs to please him. It nurses the sincere and heartfelt intention to live for him, not for oneself, but for him![34]

Any vision of God that does not fill their lives with this habit of mind will be inadequate.

It is interesting that the Bible does not focus on "getting faith" but simply assumes that people have faith. Therefore, Scripture instead probes the object of our faith. Everyone trusts in something or someone. The object of our faith determines how we live and the decisions we make. Consequently, Christian women whose epistemology weaves together the analytical and the personal insist that they must be clear about the object of their faith. The preacher's task is to make the biblical images of God concrete for these listeners, at least as concrete as the images emanating from the television screen or from magazine ads. Above all else, the preacher must convey clearly and concretely the multifaceted but unified vision of God as the trustworthy object of faith for salvation and for daily life. Only then can these women begin to live by faith.

Preaching Effectively to Diverse Spiritualities

Women have different spiritual longings and logjams, depending on the way they know what they know. The preacher may conclude that reaching some will necessarily lead to neglecting others. In a sense, that may be true. But it is not necessarily the whole story.

As noted earlier, preaching from the lives of the people presented in the Scriptures can connect a biblical vision of God to women's lives today. In particular, women are stimulated when they hear preaching based on the lives of great women in the Bible. They are able to enter into the struggles of Esther, who had to risk her life and defy a king to save her people (Esther 4). Some women can identify with the widow of Zarephath, being asked first to share with a stranger the only food in the house, then later being deprived (for a time) of her only son (1 Kings 17). Others identify with Hannah in her infertility (1 Samuel 1–2). Still others take note of Deborah's style of leadership (Judges 4–5) or the way Huldah used her prophetic gift (2 Kings 22). Phoebe, Priscilla, Junia, and others are New Testament models for Christian service (Romans 16). Mary helps women put motherhood in its proper place in their lives (Matt. 12:46–50). Both Mary of Bethany (John 12) and the sinful woman of Luke 7 teach women about worshiping the Lord, even as the Syrophoenician woman teaches them about faith in times of crisis (Matthew 15). Obviously, no congregation wants a steady diet of sermons on biblical women. Yet many congregations never hear these stories, and thus women are deprived of the modeling and teaching that reaches them best.[35]

In the biblical encounters of genuine people with difficult problems, faith and the object of faith are tested. Rationally, we understand that faith needs testing or exercising to grow strong, yet faith can be lost when tested. This risk sometimes causes preachers to avoid passages of Scripture that might create questions in listeners' minds about God's dealings with people. Biblical narratives and teachings are sometimes "sanitized" so as not to threaten people's faith. Although that is laudable, it is unrealistic. People live in the real world, and that fact challenges faith every day. They need the message of the Bible that God does work for good, though not always in ways that seem good at the time (Isa. 55:8–9).

Take, for example, the widow of Zarephath (1 Kings 17). She and her son faced starvation. She had only a handful of flour and a bit of oil left with which to make one last meal before they would die. While gathering firewood to bake that last small bit of bread, she was interrupted by a stranger from Israel, the prophet Elijah. He asked her for something to eat. She answered, "As the LORD your God lives, I . . . have . . . only a handful of flour in a bin, and a little oil in a jar; and see, I am gathering a couple of sticks that I may go in and prepare it for myself and my son, that we may eat it, and die" (v. 12). Elijah responded, "Do not fear; go and do as you have said, but make me a small cake from it first, and bring it to me; and afterward make some for yourself and your son. For thus says the LORD God of Israel: 'The bin of flour shall not be used up, nor shall the jar of oil run dry, until the day the LORD sends rain on the earth'" (vv. 13–14). For this woman, Elijah's request was a major test of faith in a God whom she considered a foreign god, not one of her Sidonian gods. In that moment, she had to decide whether to do as the prophet asked, diminishing her few resources even further, or decide that he was a fool and ignore his request.

Whether or not faith results from a challenge to give away the last of all we have, in the end it depends on our vision of God. The widow of Zarephath knew enough to call Elijah's God "LORD," the name of Israel's covenant-keeping God. For her, it was enough to know that the God of Israel was involved, and it generated faith to do what the prophet asked.

In preaching about faith, it is not enough to preach "the faith," a body of doctrine to be believed. Nor is it enough to preach "simple trust" without a strong biblical vision of God as the mighty and trustworthy One. Doctrine and trust are two sides of the coin of faith. Neither is enough without the other because faith must be clear about its object (God) before it can be confident enough to trust.

The Hebrew and Greek words translated "faith" in both the Old and New Testaments have a twofold application: They can be translated as "faith" or as "faithful." When Habakkuk looked around at conditions in Israel, he was appalled. The people of God were perverting justice on every hand, and the prophet cried out to God for judgment against the evildoers. But when God responded with his plan to deal with them by delivering them into the hands of the wicked Chaldeans, Habakkuk was even more upset. He asked, "Why do you look on those who deal treacherously, and hold your tongue when the wicked devours one more righteous than he?" (Hab. 1:13). At that point the prophet stationed himself on a rampart, determined to wait and see how God would answer him. The answer from God included the words "the just shall live by faith" (Hab. 2:4). New Testament writers picked up these words—Paul in Romans 1:17 and Galatians 3:11, and the writer of the letter to the Hebrews (10:38): "the just shall live by faith." Some scholars have rendered these passages as "the just shall live by *faith in God's faithfulness.*" Faith grows as our knowledge of the faithfulness of our God grows.

Preaching is a call to faith. But faith in what? The Bible is clear that it is faith in a faithful God. That calls for both a knowledge of the Holy One and a confidence in him. This is the essence of Christian spirituality. Preaching to women of all epistemologies calls for preaching a faithful vision of God that listeners are able to trust. Only then will they be able to love him with all their minds.

It is impossible to conserve for the kingdom of God every man or woman who enters a church door. Women, like men, are sinners who can be stubborn and willful. All of us—men and women alike—are like sheep who easily go astray, seeking our own way. Bringing these sheep back to God is what the gospel is about. As we understand how different people process knowledge (and thus spiritual teaching), we can perhaps reach some who might otherwise, like Carol Christ, leave orthodox Christianity. In *The Goddess Revival,* Aida Besançon Spencer and her colleagues comment that

> all around the world, women and men—many feeling disenfranchised within Christian circles or disillusioned by the liberalism within much of the church, many simply seeking answers to the world's ecological crisis and/or remedies for their own vacuous spiritual states—are turning to paganism in its many expressions: witchcraft, earth-centered worship, worship of the pre-Christian god/dess in his/her many forms.[36]

We cannot stop every person from making that move. We can, however, do our utmost to match truth to life as we understand the minds and hearts of those who listen to our words on Sunday morning. The vision of God we paint from week to week will help or hinder women from learning to love God with all their minds.

Summing Up the Chapter

- The question of women's spirituality (how they know and relate to God) cannot be separated from epistemology (how we know what we know).
- Silent women are best reached and taught by frequent contact and conversation with women who love God with their minds and talk about his empowering presence in their lives.
- Women who have been taught that passivity is the proper and godly role for Christian women may neglect to stir up the gifts of God within them for ministry, somehow believing that to do so puts others at risk.
- If preachers want to communicate to subjective knowers, they will use narrative biblical literature, especially the narratives of women's experiences.
- Preaching to procedural knowers means preaching a vision of God adequate to every circumstance in life. It is that vision of God that enables them to love him with all their minds as well as with all their hearts and souls.
- Constructed knowers, more than any other knowers, are seriously occupied with the moral and spiritual dimensions of their lives. These women are passionate knowers with a capacity for attentive love.
- Faith can pose problems for parishioners who listen to your sermons each week. Some wrestle with the difference between *knowing* and *believing*. Others struggle with the fact of many different ideas about God, wondering which one is correct. Still others wonder merely how much faith is enough faith to get them to heaven. Some find faith difficult, even impossible, in the face of their life experiences.

- In preaching about faith, it is not enough to preach "the faith," a body of doctrine to be believed. Nor is it enough to preach "simple trust" without a strong biblical vision of God as the mighty and trustworthy One. Doctrine and trust are two sides of the same coin of faith. Neither is enough without the other because faith must be clear about its subject (God) before it can be confident enough to trust.
- Preaching is a call to faith. But faith in what? The Bible is clear that it is faith in a faithful God. That calls for both a knowledge of the Holy One and a confidence in him. Preaching to women of all epistemologies calls for preaching a faithful vision of God that listeners are able to trust. Only then will they be able to love him with all their minds.

Questions to Ponder

- How do you "conceive and speak of God"?
- How can you encourage a spiritual formation in women that is anchored in Scripture and becomes a permanent habit of the heart, soul, and mind?
- How is the preaching task essential to that spiritual formation?
- What difference ought our vision of God make in our daily lives?
- In what way should that vision of God translate into a solid biblical spirituality?

7

Women and Issues of Power

Years ago when speaking in a large church in upstate New York, I used an illustration drawn from my sewing machine. Before continuing with the application of that illustration to my message, I paused and said (as an aside), "That illustration was my sweet revenge for all the football stories I've had to listen to over the years." I wasn't prepared for the response that came: first a ripple of laughter, then a roar of applause as many of the women stood to their feet, clapping vigorously.

As noted in chapter 2, competitive games (especially rough contact sports) in which one team will necessarily lose to the other team are not particularly interesting to many women. The power struggle on the field for dominance and ultimately for victory may spike the adrenalin of some spectators but may leave others feeling less than comfortable.

Yet competitive team sports have strong historical and sociological importance to many men and women in society. Prior to the development of the factory system and the availability of jobs away from the home, families lived and worked together as an economic unit. As a result, men had many opportunities to demonstrate their strength and courage in the presence of their wives and children. Wives, sons, and daughters saw their husbands and fathers at work in the fields or in small shops attached to the home. Children (especially sons) learned to hunt and fish or to clear land and build barns by working alongside their fathers, who passed on the skills needed for survival. But as the Industrial Revolution carried fathers away from home to jobs in factories or offices, families no longer witnessed the strength, skills, and knowledge that men brought to their work. Men lost an important contact with their children, and families lost a level of appreciation for a father's work. Furthermore, jobs in factories or offices did not require the physical strength needed on a farm or in a home-based business such as carpentry or blacksmithing. The personal identity of men was challenged by the Industrial Revolution and throughout the nineteenth and twentieth centuries.

Some men tried to recapture what they had lost by being authoritarian in the home. Others tried to regain feelings of manhood by bringing the tactics and vocabulary of warfare into corporate life, where they could fight battles and crush opponents. For many, competitive team sports in which men can display or admire physical strength and skill have become important substitutes for a life most men no longer live in our industrial/technological society. Thus, I acknowledge the importance of football illustrations in a sermon! At the same time, not every listener is reached by the same illustration. Just as the men in that congregation in upstate New York must have scratched their heads (or more likely yawned) at my sewing machine illustration, many women find a steady diet of sports stories equally boring.

What is a preacher to do? Is it enough to try to balance the number of sports and non-sports illustrations? Of course not. Illustrations point to a deeper issue of power and how you, the preacher, think about power. It is impossible to preach an effective sermon without invoking power in some form to influence your listeners' lives. Whether you talk about God's power to overturn sin (used against the world, the flesh, or the devil), or the power of love to win out over evil, or the power of faith to move mountains, or even just the power of positive thinking, in one way or another you bring some kind of power into most sermons. If there is no power to change present confusing or hurtful situations, listeners may decide there is no point in listening to the sermon. Reflect on the sermons you have preached in the past year. What kind of power did you invoke to help listeners put what you said into practice?

We seldom think about power. We assume it. It is like the air we breathe. C. P. Snow in *Corridors of Power* noted that "to make the real decisions, one's got to have the real power."[1] Our personal experience corroborates that. Anyone who has been given a responsibility but not the power to carry it out has been asked to do the impossible. In *Power and the Corporate Mind,* Abraham Zalenick and Manfred F. R. Ket DeVries observed that power "is what makes people tick, organizations run, and executives manage."[2] Power is also what gives sermons an edge, a raison d'etre. It gives listeners a reason to go to church.

So the question remains. What is your attitude toward power? Some have a "winners and losers" way of thinking about power. Others see power as God's *energeia* to get things done. Whatever your view of power, it will influence not only your sermon illustrations but also the sermons themselves.

Preaching the Great Commandment includes enabling women to love God with all their strength.[3] Strength in the Bible means having the ability, force, might, or power to accomplish something.[4] Christian women should love God not merely emotionally but also with actions that use abilities, strength, or power. The woman who is not encouraged to develop God-given skills and interests for use in God's kingdom cannot love God with all her strength because it has not been fully developed. Yet for some women, the use of strength poses a dilemma arising from what they have been taught about gender and power.

Gender and Power

Entire books have been written about the relationship between gender and power. This chapter examines only three issues that have implications for preaching: (1) how men and women may differ in their view of power; (2) how many women feel about power and its abuse; and (3) the relationship between sin and the use or negation of power.

Do Men and Women View Power in the Same Way?

When examining men's and women's attitudes toward power, some researchers found that men are more likely to view power as a discrete quantity. There is only a certain amount of it: "If I have this much power and I give some of it to you, I will have less power." Power is the ebb and flow of competitive bargaining in the workplace or in politics.[5] Leaders facilitate the exchange of goods by calculating interests or maneuvering for strategic advance. Men talk about business teamwork in terms of sports rules and competitive analogies, role clarity and tight controls.[6] The object of the game is to come out on top, to win, not lose.

According to these same researchers, women, on the other hand, tend to view power as something that increases as it is shared. A woman who gives power to another person does not necessarily feel that her own power is diminished by sharing it. To most women, power expands as others gain it. Management pioneer Mary Parker Follet sees women's understanding of the use of power in stark contrast to a bargaining or competitive use: There is a way to use power "in which neither side has . . . to sacrifice anything."[7] Women focus on relationship—valuing the autonomy of individuals, empowering others, and "connectedness without hierarchy."[8] Of course, this is not true of every woman in the workplace or in the church, just as competitive uses of power are not true of every man. Men who were mentored on the job by women share power much more freely than men who were mentored by men. Women who were mentored by men are more likely to guard their power as something they will lose if they share it. Chapter 8 explores in greater detail women's understanding of power and its legitimate use, as well as the challenge these attitudes toward power present for preachers.

How Do Most Women Feel about Power?

Beyond those differing attitudes toward power, more important is the fact that many women fear power. Recently, a friend asked me to meet her for lunch. After we ordered our food, she began: "I'm forty-one years old, and nothing in my life is the way I always thought it would be. When I finished college, I was sure I'd get married and have children. But I'm still single. And I'm having to face the fact that I may stay single. So I work. I recently changed jobs. The old job was boring. There was no challenge to my creativity, and after four years in that position, I knew I had to get out or die. Now I'm doing something I enjoy, but I realize that while the work is going well, in some ways I'm not prepared inside my head for the responsibilities of directing this innovative program. I don't know where to go from here."

As we talked, it became clear that she was struggling with power on several levels. On one level, she had an opportunity to use power on the job and was not sure she knew how to wield it in good ways. On another level, she was blocked from much decision-making in her position by a senior-level man (not connected to her position in any way) who wanted to call the shots for her. On yet another level, she was asking what it meant to be a Christian woman exercising power in the workplace: Was it legitimate from a biblical understanding of power to move forward and make decisions on her own? One power struggle was within herself concerning her ability to use power responsibly. Another power struggle was with another person who wanted to control her work, even though she was the director of the program. The third struggle was with the meaning and demands of her role as a Christian woman. She feared that as a Christian woman perhaps she should not do what her position called for. Many women struggle with the same three problems when placed in situations calling for the exercise of power: Do I have the ability to do this right? Do I have the strength to stand up to others to get this job done? Do I have God's permission to exercise power as a Christian woman?

How would you answer those questions from the pulpit for the women who listen to you? You might legitimately shy away from the first question because different people have different abilities to lead and innovate. But before you duck and run from the question, step back and ask yourself how you empower listeners from the pulpit to use power in godly ways. My friend's question had to do with the right way to use the power of her position to benefit others. Do you have a well-thought-out theology of the godly use of power that you could expound from the pulpit? Have your parishioners heard you discuss power from the Scriptures so that they do not have to wonder how to use their power on the job?

What about the second question: How can my friend stand up to the interference of someone above her who is not in the chain of command over her program? Jesus had to deal with interference from the Jewish religious authorities who wanted to control his person and his work. When and how did he stand up to them? What understanding of power governed his actions? Do your people know when and how they can stand up to those who unlawfully attempt to control their legitimate use of power?

Then there is the third question: How does being a Christian woman affect the use of power? This is land mine territory in many churches, and an extended discussion of the issue is not within the purview of this book. Yet every preacher, wittingly or otherwise, by implication or direct statement, teaches men and women about the boundaries of their social roles. Have you thought concretely about how your own beliefs about gender roles affect women? If so, have you helped them understand how they are to use the power necessary to their tasks in ways that honor God?

Beyond the fear of power in their own hands, most women also fear the *abuse* of power in the hands of others. Chapter 4 examined women who live in silence, in terror of the capricious use of power by those on whom they depend. We also looked at women who as passive or received knowers reached a state of crisis of confidence in their authority figures. This created in them a rebellion against all exercise of power over them by external authorities.

Power can be abused in many ways. We easily recognize it when it is blatant but may miss it when it is well disguised. We see it clearly in crimes against children and women such as incest or rape, but we may not see it for what it is when it is masked in language that passes it off as something moral or good. From the beginning of creation, men and women have been tricked and seduced by power. Adam and Eve sinned in the Garden of Eden when they decided to take the route that would make them "like God." It was out of his own firsthand experience that Satan tempted them with what seemed "good." He had also felt the siren call of power and had fallen from heaven's glory when he had answered that call. Ever since, he has used power—often well disguised—to tempt men and women. In fact, even a positive biblical doctrine can be skewed when it is infested with an abuse of power. For example, the Puritans (among others) believed that they could judge a person's faithfulness to God by his or her prosperity.[9] This made it a duty to strive for wealth, the sign of God's approval for faithfulness. Yet the act of striving for wealth opened the door to the abuse of power over others.[10]

When the Industrial Revolution took fathers out of the household and put them into a distant workplace, the emerging doctrine of separate spheres was quickly baptized into the Christian faith as dogma and has become virtually impossible to overturn. Out of it have flowed many abuses of power within families. A great deal of abuse enters Christian homes through a faulty understanding of "headship."[11] Most scholars who read Ephesians 5:21–33 would say that wives are to submit to their husbands but that husbands are called by God to sacrifice their own will to power in order to bring their wives to perfection. They are to love their wives to the same degree that they love their own flesh and care for it. There is no room in any of this for the abuse of power. In Christ there is neither male nor female; we are all one in Christ.

Is Sin the Same for Men and Women?

A third gender factor concerns the relationship between power and sin. Theologian Valerie Saiving defined the concept of sin as "the unjustified concern of the self for its own power and prestige."[12] She then argued that the life experiences of men and women are so different that such a definition of sin may not be equally applicable to men and women. In particular, the maternal role forces women to transcend their own development. As noted in chapter 3, boys are brought up to take charge of their futures, to be winners in the game of life. This is not true in the same way for many girls. Saiving concluded that while sin for men may be "the will to power" (to borrow Friedrich Nietzsche's words), sin for women may more accurately be a constellation of small things that add up to an underdevelopment or negation of the self. The "small things" are not really small if considered in the light of biblical teaching. The list includes the lack of an organizing center or focus in a woman's life so that she concerns herself with the trivial. Other "small things" include depending on others for self-definition and tolerating mediocrity at the expense of excellence.[13] Saiving's catalog of "sin" for women is certainly not true of every woman. For some women the will to power is indeed the driving force in their lives. And while many churches may have some women who are characterized by "triviality, distractibility, and diffuseness," many Christian women are focused on what is not trivial. In the same way, not all men are driven by the will to power.

Yet as also noted in chapter 3, in many women there is a debilitating underdevelopment or negation of the self. In the study of gender and self-esteem in nine Canadian Bible colleges, strong differences between men and women emerged in measures of self-confidence. While men's general self-confidence at times leads them to overestimate their abilities, it also leads them to attempt more things, giving them more opportunities to increase their skills and be rewarded. Women, on the other hand, tend to underestimate their abilities. Consequently, they more easily limit their world and their potential.[14] The relevant question is whether a woman's denial of her gifts and abilities and her reluctance to attempt new things—consequences of the wrong kind of selflessness—represent another form of sin, the sin of refusing to become the person God designed her to be.

This leads to one of the paradoxes of the Christian life. On the one hand, Jesus said, "If anyone desires to come after Me, let him deny himself, and take up his cross, and follow Me. For whoever desires to save his life will lose it, but whoever loses his life for My sake will find it" (Matt. 16:24–25). In the last hours before his crucifixion, Jesus reminded his followers that the seed that falls into the ground and dies is the seed that will bring forth fruit (John 12:24). On the other hand, Jesus also said, "From everyone to whom much has been given, much will be required" (Luke 12:48 NRSV). Then there is Paul's reminder to Timothy to "stir up the gift of God which is in you" (2 Tim. 1:6). How are Christian women to view the gifts God has given them to build up Christ's kingdom? And how are preachers to enable people to stir up the gifts of God within them—without also stirring up the ungodly will to power? What is a legitimate self-denial that does not negate God's calling and gifts? And what is a legitimate desire to achieve much for God and his glory?

Chapter 6 began with lines from a poem by English missionary Amy Carmichael, the founder of the Dohnavur Fellowship in India. In it she prayed that God would keep her "from fearing when I should aspire, from faltering when I should climb higher." Is this a legitimate prayer for women to pray? How do you empower your listeners to pray that and the final lines of the poem: "Let me not sink to be a clod: / Make me Thy fuel, Flame of God"?

Jesus and Power

Jesus understood the contagious infection of power. On the evening before his death, he overheard a conversation that bothered him greatly. His followers were arguing about who among them was the greatest. Luke and John both recorded Jesus' admonition to his disciples that night: "The greatest among you must become like the youngest, and the leader like one who serves" (Luke 22:26 NRSV). Jesus had to set his followers straight about issues of power. Followers of Christ are to be marked by service, he said, not by the exercise of power. Only a few hours later, after his arrest, Jesus had opportunities to use his own divine power against his enemies, but he chose instead to die without defending himself. Power, it would appear, is not what the Christian life is about.

But although Jesus knew the dangers of power and called his followers to deny its siren call, he also knew the danger of *powerlessness*. He preached against those who consistently took advantage of the powerless (Matthew 23). He went further: He empowered many who were powerless. He challenged people's contentment with the status quo, turning simple fishermen and a tax collector into apostles for God. He enabled women to find their voices in his service. He broke the shackles of demon possession, setting people free to serve God with clear minds and cleansed hearts. This is a different use of power.

Furthermore, just before his ascension to the Father in glory, Jesus told his followers that they would "receive power when the Holy Spirit has come upon you" and that they would become witnesses to him, the Word made flesh (Acts 1:8). In the next chapter, Luke notes that women as well as men were in that group upon whom God's power fell (Acts 2:17–18). God has given Christians a particular kind of power, and Jesus was explicit about the use of that power: It was to be used to witness to the gospel throughout the world ("in all Judea and Samaria, and to the end of the earth" [1:8]). That power is given to enable us to accomplish God's purposes in the world.

Yet many women, gifted by God, do not develop their gifts for witness and ministry because they do not believe they can or should. Christian women who do shoulder the task of preparation for service to Jesus Christ sometimes find that male colleagues question their "right" to pursue biblical and theological studies in a Christian college or seminary. In some schools, certain courses are closed to them. They may have professors who do not take them seriously. Administrators sometimes write them off as being in school merely as "husband hunters." It is not surprising that their self-confidence falters or that they fall back into what Saiving called "the underdevelopment or negation of the self."

How Does This Apply to Preaching?

Men and women have differing understandings of power (its use and abuse), and that can affect how they hear even an illustration based on a football game or a sewing machine. How can you preach so that all God's people hear a message of power undistorted by human sinfulness? It may be helpful to examine God's use of power in order to understand godly uses of power. While Scripture, from the opening lines of Genesis to the final chapter of Revelation, talks about God and his power, we find a kind of synopsis of God's uses of power in Psalm 136.

The psalmist begins with a clear vision of the biblical God: the LORD, the God of gods, the Lord of lords, who is the covenant-keeping God of power but also the God of goodness and mercy.[15] Having established the LORD God as the object of praise in the psalm, the writer then illustrates four ways in which our great God uses power:

- The first illustration takes us back to Genesis 1 and the creation of the heavens and earth (vv. 5–9): God uses power to bring order from chaos and to provide the means by which his creatures can not only survive but also thrive.
- The second way in which God uses power takes us from Egypt to the Promised Land (vv. 10–22): In this case, God uses power to redeem people from slavery.
- But interwoven in those same verses is the third way in which God uses power: He destroys those who oppose God's purposes for his people (vv. 10–22).
- The fourth way God uses power takes us into the present: God provides for his own (vv. 23–25).

It is legitimate to use power to bring order from chaos so that God's creatures can thrive as well as survive. It is legitimate to use power to free people from whatever binds or enslaves them. It is legitimate to use power to stand up to those who oppose God and his purposes on this earth. And it is legitimate to use power to provide for the people of God.

As you preach any text, you may want to evaluate the way you talk about power in the light of God's use of power. Because power invades virtually every sermon in one form or another, and because listeners need to understand and live under God's power in their lives, you may want to ask if the power you are invoking in a sermon resembles God's use of power. Is it power used to bring order from chaos or to create means by which God's people can thrive? Is it power used to redeem people from slavery? Is it power used to hold back the forces that work to destroy the people of God? Is it power used to care for all the people of God?

Both men and women live in a world in which power structures dominate their daily lives. They sometimes experience power used abusively against them. In business, powerful people steal other people's ideas and use them as their own. Or top executives pocket huge bonuses as the "little people" struggle to make a living. In politics, power easily corrupts good people and may defeat the best people. At times, churches suffer as powerful deacons chase a godly pastor from the pulpit or as a pastor uses power to abuse people in the congregation. In some homes, children suffer sexual abuse at the hands of a powerful adult, or a wife is battered by a physically stronger husband. Christian men and women in the workplace and in the community see the abuse of power blighting their lives. How are they to understand the godly use of power? It is in the biblical vision of God that listeners can find answers to that question.

Psalm 136 reveals one more ingredient of the godly use of power, one that is particularly important for women to hear: God *always* wraps his use of power in divine love. The psalm is antiphonal. One half of the congregation stated the facts about God, and in every verse the other half of the congregation responded with the antiphon: God's lovingkindness is everlasting. God's love endures forever. When God uses his power, love controls every act. Women (and men) need to hear that the power of this world is not the power of our God or of his Christ. The power that manipulates desires (whether for goods or for God) is not from God. The power from God is a spiritual power that every believer receives. It is the power to overcome evil, to resist temptation, to serve God. And just as God wrapped every use of power in divine love, so we—men and women alike—must wrap every use of power in love. Throughout the pages of Scripture we meet patriarchs, judges, priests, kings, prophets, and apostles who struggled against becoming children of the lesser god, power. They desired the power from God, a power that always works for good.

God's power is given to women as well as to men for the blessing of the world. Women need to know that they too have been empowered by God. But most women understand intuitively the danger of corrupted power, and they shy away from using power. In the process, they may fail to use God's gifts and fall short of fulfilling God's calling. Women need to know that they have gifts and are indwelt by God's mighty Spirit for the purpose of serving Christ and others in the world. Only then can they love God with all their strength.

Summing Up the Chapter

- It is impossible to preach an effective sermon without invoking power in some form to influence your listeners' lives. If there is no power to change present confusing or hurtful situations, listeners may decide there is no point in listening to the sermon.

- When examining men's and women's attitudes toward power, some researchers found that men are more likely to view power as a discrete quantity. There is only a certain amount of it: "If I have this much power and I give some of it to you, I will have less power." Women, on the other hand, tend to view power as something that increases in quantity as it is shared.
- Power can be abused in many ways. We easily recognize it when it is blatant but may miss it when it is well disguised.
- In many women there is a debilitating underdevelopment or negation of the self.
- It is possible that a woman's denial of her gifts and abilities and her reluctance to attempt new things—consequences of the wrong kind of selflessness—represent another form of sin, the sin of refusing to become the person God designed her to be.
- Jesus set his followers straight about issues of power: Followers of Christ are to be marked by service, not by the exercise of power.
- But Jesus also knew the danger of *powerlessness*. He preached against those who consistently took advantage of the powerless (Matthew 23), and he empowered many who were powerless.
- Jesus also promised his followers that they would "receive power when the Holy Spirit has come upon you" (Acts 1:8), enabling them to become witnesses to him. That power is given to enable us to accomplish God's purposes in the world.
- Yet many women, gifted by God, do not develop their gifts for witness and ministry because they do not believe they can or should.
- It is legitimate to use power to bring order from chaos so that God's creatures can thrive as well as survive, to free people from whatever binds or enslaves them, to stand up to those who oppose God and his purposes on this earth, and to provide for the people of God.
- Psalm 136 reveals one more ingredient of the godly use of power: God *always* wraps his use of power in divine love. Neither men nor women should use power if it is not wrapped in love.

Questions to Ponder

- Do you have a well-thought-out theology of the godly use of power that you could expound from the pulpit?

- Have your parishioners heard you discuss power from the Scriptures so that they do not have to wonder how to use their power on the job?
- Have you thought concretely about how your own beliefs about power and gender roles affect women?
- How are Christian men and women to view the gifts God has given them to build up Christ's kingdom? How can you enable people to stir up the gifts of God within them—without also stirring up the ungodly will to power?
- What is a legitimate self-denial that does not negate God's calling and gifts? What is a legitimate desire to achieve much for God and his glory?
- How can you preach so that all God's people hear a message of power undistorted by human sinfulness?

8

Leadership with a Difference

In 1994, my husband and I moved from Denver to Philadelphia to begin a new chapter in our lives. I had been invited to serve as dean of the Philadelphia center of Seminary of the East. I knew that a dean is called to lead from the middle, answering to the president and the board of trustees on the one hand, and to the faculty, staff, and students on the other hand. At that point I had not yet read much literature on leadership, so I did not have a good theoretical model in mind as I began my new calling. But I did think long and hard about the story of a soldier in the Civil War who sought to avoid being shot by wearing a Yankee coat and Rebel trousers. In the end, he was shot by the northern army in the seat of the pants and by the southern army through his jacket. As I considered the plight of that apocryphal soldier, I decided that what mattered was not the uniform I wore but staying out of a war. My task was to nurture community, not adversarial relationships. By leading from the middle, not from the top, I hoped to create a situation in which no one was "killed." I didn't know it then, but this was a very "female" approach to leadership.

Since that and subsequent moves, I have often sat in my office listening to women students wrestle with questions about effective leadership and the values they believe underlie traditional pyramidal models of leadership. Are preachers as leaders honing and using their gifts to the full extent of their ability for the glory of God? Are they employing a leadership style that is grounded in Scripture? And does the way they lead through their preaching help women to love God with all their strength? These are questions we must explore as we consider women as listeners. Other questions include how women lead when given the opportunity to do so, and whether their methods have any relevance for preaching.[1]

Before we look at these questions, it may be helpful to think about leadership in general. Peter Drucker said that "a leader is anyone who has followers."[2] Is that an adequate definition?

In business, leadership as it is practiced usually refers to people holding top positions in management—CEOs, CFOs, COOs, and so on. Some business schools now distinguish between management and leadership and teach that leadership involves providing a vision and influencing others to realize that vision. Thus, many business models now begin with vision statements.[3]

In the military, however, leadership is not about vision; it's about who is in command. According to Ronald Heifetz, the ancient linguistic root of the verb *to lead* meant "to go forth, to die." A military leader is the one who shows the way to go forth, possibly to death. He or she is "in command."

In the realm of zoology, the leader is the biggest, the fastest, the most beautiful, or the most assertive animal, bird, or fish. Leadership is not about vision or command; it's about dominance. And in horse racing, leadership simply means "being out in front." The jockey on the lead horse is not leading anyone else; he or she is just out in front.

All of these models of leadership have two common denominators: position and power. Most of the books about leadership focus either on the personal characteristics of leaders or on the positions from which they influence history or realize their vision.

For many women, these two denominators—position and power—should be labeled "Danger: Handle with Care." They recognize the necessity of a position of sorts, and they understand the need for some kind of power. But they also know the danger inherent in both. How, then, do women look at leadership? What differences have researchers detected between women's leadership styles and traditional understandings of leadership?

When Women Lead

John Naisbitt and Patricia Aburdene, in their book *Megatrends 2000*, looked at changes that had already taken place in the United States and predicted major changes to come during the 1990s. They called chapter 7 of the book "The 1990s: Decade of Women in Leadership" and stated that leadership styles would have to change because the world had changed. It is much more difficult to "manage" work going on inside people's heads than to manage the work of their hands. To succeed in the new work environments, Naisbitt concluded that the effective leader for the twenty-first century would have to be "open, ethical, empowering, and inspiring . . . through honest, ethical management."[4] Now that the 1990s, the "Decade of Women in Leadership," are part of history, we must ask, How have women provided leadership in secular arenas? Have they brought a different leadership style that in any way fits with Naisbitt's prediction?

In 1998, Cindy Simon Rosenthal published her findings on the leadership styles of women and men elected to state legislatures in several American states, comparing men with women as they chaired committees.[5] She found that, in general, women differ from men in their personal motivations and goals, in traits characteristic of their style, and in areas such as sharing power. The women in this study worked through interpersonal networks and cooperating parties. They listened, educated, and empowered others. They facilitated learning, working to transform others. On the other hand, the legislative men in this study were leader-centered, working in hierarchies, pitting competing interests against one another. They led by directing, by bargaining with others, by exercising power over others, and by brokering exchanges.

The differences between these two leadership styles have been aptly compared to the difference between the octopus and the goose: The octopus has one central brain and many hands to do its bidding. In contrast, the goose sniffs fall in the air and shares the vision of the South with the gaggle. Once in the air, the leader of the V-formation breaks the wind resistance for the flock. Eventually, the lead goose tires and goes to the end of the V, with another goose taking its place.[6]

The male model of leadership in Rosenthal's study resembled an octopus: a pyramid with top-down directives or instructions to others. The male legislators in the study dealt with winners and losers, with conflict and competition as necessary parts of the system. The question was, Who gets what at whose expense? In most states, legislative decisions are "divide-the-dollar" competitions in which self-interest for one's own constituency overshadows the broader common good. This has been called "the classic sea of transactional leadership."[7] Others call it "pork-barrel politics."

In contrast, Rosenthal found that the women legislators emphasized mutuality and shared problem-solving with win-win strategies. In this study, women chairpersons were far more motivated by people's needs and policy goals than were men. Women wanted to know who would be helped or hurt by a particular law. As women gained experience in leadership, they cared less about the pocketbook issues of a few constituents and more about the health and welfare of people in general in the nation. Women leaders more frequently consulted others and shared strategic information. The women in this study saw power as something to use to support and cooperate, not to dominate. Their view was "power to" (get things done) rather than "power over."

In studies of businesses, management researchers found that men conceive of management as rules, roles, and controls. Women managers, on the other hand, focus on relationships and connectedness without hierarchy. Other researchers found that women use power for the purpose of nurturing rather than controlling. Business researcher Judy Rosener concluded that women in business are more likely than men to encourage participation, to empower others, and to celebrate the worth of other people.[8] The study conducted by Jean Lipman-Blumen and her colleagues of more than five thousand American managers (2,041 women, 3,126 men) found that women perceived themselves as decidedly less competitive than their male counterparts perceived themselves.[9] The Claremont Graduate University Institute for Advanced Studies in Leadership cited evidence that "women use their power in more socially constructive ways within organizations than do their male counterparts. More specifically, they tend to use power to achieve organizational goals, rather than to enhance their own political strength."[10] The same report noted that "women at the highest corporate levels are decidedly more likely than their male peers to trust the implementation of their vision to others. This suggests women's growing comfort with delegating and empowering others."[11]

In general, women view power as a means to promote change, whereas men tend to view power as a means of having influence over other people. Women managers are more likely to use and share power, while men base power on position or ability to reward or punish. David McClelland argues that women view power as highly interdependent, interpersonal, indirect, and contextual. Men are more likely to see power in personal, direct, analytical, and aggressive terms.[12]

What about studies that look at leadership styles in the context of the church? In 1993, Edward Lehman[13] published the results of an extensive study of leadership styles among clergy in four mainline Protestant denominations.[14] He found that some dimensions of ministry style were more gender-specific than others, with men and women clergy differing consistently in four areas:

- a willingness or unwillingness to use power over a congregation
- a desire to empower a congregation to manage its own life
- a preference for rational structures when dealing with ethical issues
- legalistic tendencies when dealing with ethical issues

The clergy*men* were more prone than the clergy*women* to use power over a congregation, to prefer rational structures for decision-making, and to approach ethics legalistically.[15] The clergywomen were more likely than the clergymen to try to give a congregation power over its own affairs.

Overall, research indicates that the majority of women who lead have a more collegial leadership style. Not all women do, of course. In business, women who have been mentored by men usually lead like men, as noted in chapter 7. On the other hand, studies show that men who were mentored by women in business have many of the traits of women's leadership style. The style is not inherently gender-specific. But it is clearly different.

Sally Helgesen, writing about women's ways of leadership, called her book *The Female Advantage:* She concluded that women's leadership style has an advantage because it is more effective.[16] People—particularly women—are more creative and happy when they feel secure in a web of inclusion than when they feel as if they are at the bottom of the food chain. Such a style is especially advantageous for Christian women because it more closely resembles the apostle Paul's image of the body and Jesus' description of the behavior of those who follow him. How does this image fit with other recent research on leadership theory?

Leadership with a Difference

In 1994, Harvard leadership professor Ronald Heifetz proposed a nontraditional definition of leadership. He asked whether it is possible to lead from the middle. Heifetz raised the question: "What is the difference between saying that 'leadership means influencing the community to follow the leader's vision' and saying, 'leadership means influencing the community to face its problems'?"[17] He pointed out that in the first case the mark of leadership is *influence:* A leader gets people to accept his or her vision, and the community looks to the leader to address any problems. In the second case, the mark of leadership is *progress on problems:* A leader mobilizes people to face their problems. In the first, the leader is out front occupying a position of authority. But Heifetz insisted (and I agree) that *true* leadership is not a top-down arrangement based on personal charisma. Leadership is an activity that can be done from anywhere in the pecking order because leaders are needed whenever there are problems people need to address.

Simply put, leading means enabling people to address their problems satisfactorily. More often than not, the problems surface when there is a gap between what people believe is right and what they experience. Whenever people become aware of a gap between their ideals and their reality, or between their practices and their values, they have a problem. The person who comes alongside (from anywhere in the pecking order) and helps individuals lessen the gap between values and reality is a leader.[18]

This is a different model of leadership. Or is it? A leader who comes alongside others dealing with a problem is a person who can paint a vision of the convergence of values and reality, who can influence others to work on their problems because it is possible to close the gap between values and reality. But doing this does not necessarily mean being out in front.[19] Leadership is the process of bringing people to a point of having to face their problems[20] and to deal with them. *And that is what preaching is about.* A preacher is constantly working with the gaps between ideals and realities, between practices and values.

Look at the ways Jesus modeled this kind of leadership. In John 3, Jesus led Nicodemus to face the reality that without the new birth all his religious practices as a Pharisee would not allow him to see the kingdom of God. In John 4, Jesus led a Samaritan woman to acknowledge her "irregular" domestic life and to seek to know how best to worship God. In John 5, Jesus used the healing of the lame man at Bethesda's pool to confront unbelieving Jews with their unbelief. Jesus constantly worked with the gaps between people's ideals and their realities, between their practices and their values.

Leadership means learning how to address the conflicts in values that people hold, or to shrink the gap between the values they say they stand for and the reality they live out each day. At times leadership means orchestrating conflict in order to bring to light the internal contradictions in men's and women's lives. Until people see these internal contradictions for what they are, they will not make changes in their values, beliefs, or behaviors.

Chapter 2 explored briefly the problem faced by a pregnant teenager whose boyfriend urged her to abort because he did not want the responsibility of child support. Her Christian parents urged her to abort because they did not want to admit to their friends that their daughter was going to have a baby out of wedlock. On the other side, her pastor urged her to carry the baby to full term and put the child up for adoption because it is a sin to kill the unborn.

What are the contradictions in values in such a case? What are the gaps between stated values and the reality this young woman faces? What questions will a leader coming alongside this young woman have to ask in order for these gaps and contradictions to surface? How can all the principals in this case grow in their understanding of God's character and will? The parents may have convinced themselves that abortion is in their daughter's best interest, and they may be blind to their own motivations. How can they face the real reason for their advice to their daughter? The pastor may have to face the fact that while the church may have taken a strong stand against abortion, there is no program in place to help women caught in the bind of an unwanted pregnancy. Worse, perhaps the pastor's attitude is, "They made their bed—now they better lie in it." Are there gaps between his stated values and the reality the pastor must face as well? Where can this young woman turn for the physical, emotional, and spiritual support she will need if she chooses to carry the baby to full term?

Leadership means listening for the gaps between values and realities, then helping people clarify their needs and work to meet them. The hardest and most valuable tasks of leadership may be to design strategies for helping people change their attitudes, beliefs, or behaviors. Leadership is not about providing a map for the future that disregards conflicting values. Leadership is not about providing an easy way out that neglects the facts of the case. Leadership is about motivating people to face tough realities and deeply buried conflicts.

This is not the picture of leadership that most of us have. We often think of leadership in terms of maintaining the status quo or achieving a certain growth rate with as few glitches as possible. That works if the leader is running a club or a business. But that is not what the church is about. Such a picture of leadership misses the point of the Bible completely:

- The Bible is about the Lord of glory who created us to be in relationship with God and one another. (Are we?)
- The Bible is the story of humanity turning its back on its Creator, going its own way, like sheep gone astray. (Have we?)
- The Bible tells us about the Shepherd of our souls who seeks the lost and restores us to God's fold. (Do we trust him?)
- The Bible holds up a picture of redeemed creation and challenges us to live as new creatures in Christ. (What does that mean for our daily lives?)
- The Bible realistically describes the struggles we will have living as new creatures in an old-creature world of sin and death. (Do we take this reality seriously?)
- The Bible calls us to model our new nature before a watching world. (Do we do this?)

Preaching involves addressing these central themes of Scripture in the context of the problems of everyday existence in a fallen world. The preacher is a leader who is able to locate the disparities between values and circumstances and then to work with people in the pew to close the gaps through the application of biblical principles to values, beliefs, and behaviors.

But leading people to maturity in Christ may mean letting go of some traditional notions of leadership and practicing some of the "feminine" leadership styles. When women lead, much of the focus is on listening to understand the issues and then educating in ways that transform situations. Women understand power not as a finite quantity but as something that can be shared with others. So they empower others. Women work within what Sally Helgesen calls "webs of inclusion."

This image of a web is remarkably similar in some respects to the dominant biblical picture of the church as a body. This is our functional identity as Christians linked together. We operate as a body, not as an organization made up of many individuals of independent will. God intends that we take this image seriously. We are to function as an organism, not as an organization.

How can we do that? The church has a single living Head, Jesus Christ, who is in direct relationship with every part of the body. The apostle Paul makes this clear in Ephesians 1:22: "God placed all things under his feet and appointed him [Jesus Christ] to be head over everything for the church, which is his body" (NIV). Everything—*everything*—done in the church must affirm this reality of Christ's personal headship over the church. This means that we deny the traditional secular top-down leader role. Spiritual leaders do not control God's people directly or indirectly. They do not run the church, which is Jesus' body. Leaders have a different role.

First, human leaders are not to place anyone else in the place of God, who alone is Lord. In Matthew 20:20–28, the mother of James and John asks Jesus to give her sons positions of power in the coming kingdom. Jesus uses that moment to teach the Twelve about spiritual leadership. He specifically contrasts spiritual leadership with secular leadership, saying that "the rulers of the Gentiles lord it over them, and their high officials exercise authority over them. *Not so with you*" (vv. 25–26 NIV). In essence, Jesus states that in his church there is no room for a hierarchical organizational chart. Jesus Christ is the head.

Second, Jesus contrasts secular rule with spiritual leadership by stating that secular rulers "exercise authority over" the ruled. This implies the right and the power to control the behavior of those under them. But Christ dismisses this. The Christian model for leadership is servanthood, the antithesis of power. We as servants live our lives under the control of Jesus Christ, ministering *among*, not ministering *over,* those committed to our care. This model can work in the church only because of the supernatural headship of Jesus, who works his work in each one of us.

Third, while the goal of secular leadership is to control the behavior of others, God's purpose is to transform us so that we become more and more like Christ in our attitudes, values, emotions, commitment, and behavior. Thus, the goal of leadership is not to produce uniformity but to bring believers to deeper levels of commitment to Christ. What Christians do flows spontaneously out of who they are.

Fourth, in the church, a leader's responsibility is to provide freedom so that people can grow to be responsible. Leaders serve people by bringing them to a maturity in which they can act to close the gaps between their values and reality. Leaders do not impose a kind of maturity on them from the outside but nurture them to responsible inner maturity. When leaders lead, they lay claim to a God-given right to influence but never to coerce.

The church is a body in which every part has a strong, vital interest in the success and maturity of every other part. The body reflects the web of inclusion: A leader is not focused on leadership but on the health of every part of the body and comes alongside to empower or enable every member to become all God has designed him or her to be.

How Does This Apply to Preaching?

To lead effectively, a preacher faces four challenges, all of which directly affect the preaching ministry of the church. First, it is the leader's task to identify the gap between people's aspirations and their reality and focus attention on the specific issues created by that gap. To do this, preachers must spend time listening to people talk about what they value and what they experience. Then leaders must lead people to clarify what matters most to them. In that process, they probe for the gaps between beliefs and practices or between ideals and reality. Preaching that connects with women is preaching that understands where they are (specifically) and where they need to be (specifically).

The second challenge to the preacher is to pace the rate of challenge to existing realities, that is, to challenge current realities at a pace at which people can move to meet them. Many people are fuzzy about their problems. They lack clarity. (Recall the Huntington chart in chapter 4 that shows that people who are unclear about the gap between their ideals and their reality will deny a gap or will become cynical about it.) The preacher's task is to hold up a mirror to their lives so that they see their problems clearly. But once seen, the problem can create great stress. Pacing the rate of challenge means regulating the level of stress caused when people confront issues. A leader may see the problem clearly, but he or she may need to illumine the problem incrementally for others, giving people only as much as they can manage. Preaching for changed lives has to be paced at a rate people can absorb and live with. For example, African Americans living in the South before the Civil Rights movement lived daily with systemic racial discrimination. The minds and customs of whites could not be changed overnight. It took many incremental steps (such as sit-ins at lunch counters, marches, and boycotts) to hold up the mirror to those in power before they could see racial discrimination as evil. And it took many sermons in southern pulpits to help parishioners deal with their own hearts and the stress of social change.

The third challenge to the preacher is to keep attention focused on the relevant issues. When we are confronted with something in our lives that makes us uncomfortable, we often try to change the subject. When committees or boards are faced with a financial problem in the church, some members may change the subject by focusing on fixing blame rather than on fixing the problem. If there are lifestyle problems[21] in a congregation (and what congregation does not have these?), it becomes the delicate task of the preacher to keep attention focused on the relevant issues so that people cannot mentally and emotionally change the subject. This is not a call to preachers to harp negatively on the sins of a congregation. Keeping attention focused on the relevant issues can better be accomplished by positive messages about God's grace and will for his people in those specific areas of need.

The fourth challenge to the preacher is to keep responsibility for solving the problem on those who have the problem. Many times people expect the church or the preacher to "fix" a problem. Leaders need to help people take responsibility for their own problems. This may mean changing their expectations of their leaders. But it also means leading them to "grow up in all things into Him who is the head—Christ" (Eph. 4:15).

The apostle Paul used the points in Ronald Heifetz's model in both his preaching and his writing. He opened his first letter to the Christians at Corinth by setting the goal, the ideal, clearly before them: "To the church of God which is at Corinth, to those who are sanctified in Christ Jesus, called to be saints" (1 Cor. 1:2). But almost immediately he began addressing the realities that did not match the ideal: There were contentions among them (1:11–13), and he reminded them that he could not write to them as mature Christians "but as carnal" because the gap between their reality and the Christian ideal of sanctified people was glaring. As we walk through the Corinthian correspondence, we see Paul repeatedly affirming the ideal but challenging the present reality. At the same time we hear the apostle pacing the rate of challenge, telling them, "I fed you with milk and not with solid food; for until now you were not able to receive it, and even now you are still not able, for you are still carnal" (3:2–3). As Paul dealt with one problem, then another among the Corinthian believers, he painted the vision of holiness even as he sketched the gap between that holiness and their daily lives. And though he paced the rate of challenge to what they could receive, he did not shift the focus to things that were irrelevant. Throughout, he placed responsibility for change clearly on them.

Jesus lived out this model of leadership in both his teaching and his actions. Watch him teach and lead Mary and Martha in John 11 when Lazarus lay dead in a nearby cave. The two sisters had shown enough faith to call Jesus to come quickly when Lazarus became ill. But they did not have enough faith to imagine that Jesus could raise someone from the dead. Why did Jesus not rush to Bethany as soon as he received word of Lazarus's illness? The two sisters would not have faced the limits of their faith in Jesus without the stressful days of watching their dear brother die and mourning for him. They had to understand what they lacked in faith. Jesus paced the situation so that they would be ripe for new insights into truth.

According to John 4, Jesus planned his travel itinerary so that he would encounter a woman at a well in Sychar (Samaria). Once there, he initiated a conversation that piqued her curiosity. When she was ready for "living water," Jesus switched topics to put her under stress: He told her to get her husband. She had to admit to this stranger that she had no husband. Jesus responded, "Right! You're telling the truth. You've had five husbands, but the man you're now living with isn't your husband. You got it right" (see vv. 17–18). Only then was this woman ready for the change coming into her life. Once again we see Jesus leading through raising her stress level, identifying the gap between her reality and the ideal, pacing the challenge, and regulating the level of stress so that she was prepared for the truth he was about to give her.

In every case, Jesus worked to strengthen people in their faith and commitment. This kind of leadership builds strength in Christ's followers. Women can love God with all their strength only when they have been made strong in the Lord. Secular leadership models do not focus on building strength in followers, but a biblical model does. The objective is to enable followers to deal with their problems in ways that please God.

We see this kind of leadership in examples of men and women throughout the Bible. For example, Deborah is an excellent role model of this kind of leadership. In Judges 4, we learn that she was a prophetess, the wife of Lappidoth, and Israel's leader as its judge. As judge, she was to administer justice in the family, tribe, or nation and to protect her people with judicious military action. The Bible is clear that she combined the best qualities of an Old Testament judge, both in adjudicating disputes for her people and in strategizing when the northern tribes were overrun by the armies of Jabin, king of Canaan. For twenty years the military oppression had gone on, oppression so bad that villagers could not use the roads but had to sneak around by hidden paths and clandestine trails. Village life had ceased, and farmers were forced to thresh grain in secret at night in caves. Life and property were worth nothing. To face that crisis in the northern part of her nation, Deborah began by giving responsibility for the military action against Jabin to Barak, a northerner who knew the problem. She came alongside, identifying the gap between aspirations and reality. Barak agreed to lead the army against Jabin only if Deborah would stay at his side. It was time for her to pace the rate of challenge, regulating the level of stress she caused by appointing him as general. She saw his fear and agreed to go with him. She kept him focused on the issue when he showed fear and gave him enough input to succeed. We get a sense of Deborah in Judges 5 as she and Barak together sing praise to God: "When leaders lead in Israel, when the people willingly offer themselves, bless the LORD!" (v. 2). This woman understood what it took to lead effectively in both word and deed.

Preachers lead whenever they help others bridge the gap between their aspirations and their reality. Doing so will mean challenging their ideas and helping them see beyond their shallow goals. It will mean pacing the challenge to keep them moving forward without discouraging them. It will mean keeping the focus on the issue until people accept responsibility for it and begin to change. Preachers lead whenever they help others bridge the gap between their understanding of God and God's claims on their lives. Preachers are equipped to do that only as they are open to God's work in their own lives and have seen their own values, attitudes, and behaviors challenged and changed by the Word of God.

Preachers are leaders, given the task of leading people into truth about God and about themselves. That task includes giving them insight and the tools to love God with all their strength, that is, to use every personal ability and opportunity in the service of God and his kingdom. But leadership that accomplishes these goals is servant leadership (Matt. 20:25–28), the service of coming alongside people in the pew with a vision of God and an awareness of human sinfulness and need. You will be most effective in your preaching for long-term gain if you accept the challenges of leadership:

- the challenge to identify the gap between aspirations and reality and to focus attention on the specific issues created by that gap
- the challenge of pacing the level of stress caused when confronting issues
- the challenge of keeping people's attention focused on what needs to be fixed in their lives
- the challenge of leading people to the spiritual maturity that will enable them to deal with the gap

In general, preaching that follows this leadership style can reach both men and women. But the way the preaching is done, the biblical texts used, and the stance of the preacher can make a difference in how women hear what is said. For example, within a sermon, use women as examples of leaders who follow the biblical model. Illustrations do more than simply explain or prove or apply an idea. When illustrations are skillfully used, stereotypes in people's minds can be replaced with images that are far more constructive and biblical. For example, I have heard Haddon Robinson illustrate a point by talking about a physician. When he reaches for a pronoun to refer to this doctor, he says she. It sometimes takes people by surprise, so in that sense it grabs attention. But it does more than that: It chips away at the stereotype that only men are doctors. In Luke 15, Jesus must have shocked his first-century hearers when he told two stories back to back, both demonstrating God's seeking love for the lost. The first story is about a shepherd who lost a sheep; the second is about a woman who lost a dowry coin. How can a woman in any way model God's seeking love? Jesus illustrated his point in a way that would begin to change a stereotype held by his countrymen.

Preaching is serious business. Through preaching, men and women come to a saving faith in Jesus Christ. Preaching also paints for listeners the vision of what God wants them to be. It paints the vision of the richness and ripeness of the life God wants them to have. Then it shows them the power God gives them for living that kind of life. Only when women see that vision of God's desire and provision for them will they begin to love God with all their strength, fully using their gifts for his kingdom.

Summing Up the Chapter

- Most models of leadership have two common denominators—position and power—and most of the books about leadership focus either on the personal characteristics of leaders or on the positions from which they influence history or realize their vision.
- In general, when women lead, they differ from men in their personal motivations and goals, in traits characteristic of their style, and in areas such as sharing power.
- In a study of clergy leadership styles in four mainline denominations, a researcher found that the clergy*men* were more prone than the clergy*women* to use power over a congregation, to prefer rational structures for decision-making, and to approach ethics legalistically. The clergywomen were more likely than the clergymen to try to give a congregation power over its own affairs.
- In general, women view power as a means to promote change, whereas men tend to view power as a means of having influence

over other people. David McClelland argues that women view power as highly interdependent, interpersonal, indirect, and contextual. Men are more likely to see power in personal, direct, analytical, and aggressive terms.

- People—particularly women—are much more creative and happy when they feel secure in a web of inclusion than when they feel as if they are at the bottom of the food chain.
- Leading means enabling people to address their problems satisfactorily. The person who comes alongside (from anywhere in the pecking order) and helps individuals lessen the gap between values and reality is a leader.
- Leadership is the process of bringing people to a point of having to face their problems and to deal with them. That is what preaching is about. The preacher is constantly working with the gaps between ideals and realities, between practices and values.
- At times leadership means orchestrating conflict in order to bring to light the internal contradictions in men's and women's lives. Until people see these internal contradictions for what they are, they will not make changes in their values, beliefs, or behaviors.
- The image of a web is remarkably similar in some respects to the dominant picture of the church in Scripture as a body. This is our functional identity as Christians linked together.
- People can love God with all their strength only when they have been made strong in the Lord. Secular leadership models do not focus on building strength in followers, but a biblical model does.
- You will be most effective in preaching for long-term gain if you accept the challenges of leadership:
  - the challenge to identify the gap between aspirations and reality and to focus attention on the specific issues created by that gap
  - the challenge of pacing the level of stress caused when con fronting issues
  - the challenge of keeping people's attention focused on what needs to be fixed in their lives
  - the challenge of leading people to the spiritual maturity that will enable them to deal with the gap

Questions to Ponder

- How do you perceive the task of leadership?
- Are you more comfortable with a pyramidal leadership structure or with a web of inclusion structure for leading?
- What have you learned about women's leadership styles that might challenge traditional ways of understanding leadership?
- Does Ronald Heifetz's model of leading from the middle to enable people to deal effectively with their problems strike you as workable in your own situation?
- In what ways may your present leadership style strengthen or undermine what you say from the pulpit?

9

Women, Roles, and a Biblical Identity

Recently, I bumped into an acquaintance—a single woman—at our supermarket. "I've missed you at church!" I said. She smiled, then replied, "Well, Alice, when the pastor finishes his lengthy series on marriage and the family, I may be back. But until then you won't see me there."

Last May I chatted with a friend who also attends our church. At the end of the conversation, I said, "Will I see you in church on Sunday?" She was silent for a minute, then quietly said, "No. Ever since we lost our little boy, I can't go to church on Mother's Day. It hurts too much."

More than fifteen years ago my husband and I were part of a group from our church assigned to help with a small church plant. After a few months in the small congregation, I noticed that the adult Sunday school classes were organized around married couples, so I went to the part-time pastor and offered to teach a class for women who were alone for any reason. He discussed my offer with the deacons, then reported back to me that there was no need for such a class. I knew differently because I had become acquainted with several single women who attended the worship service but not the adult Bible study classes preceding it. Their needs continued to go unmet.

A few years later, in the same growing church, I talked with the leaders of ministries to women about scheduling a small group outreach or Bible study in the evenings for women who work outside the home. I was told that all the women in the church were full-time homemakers, and there was no reason to start something for working women. The daytime activities were adequate. Several months later, however, a questionnaire filled out by women who attended the worship services revealed that nearly 70 percent of the women in the congregation worked outside the home.

What made the women who were alone invisible to the deacons? Or what made the women who worked outside the home invisible to the leaders of the women's ministries in that church?

In all these encounters, the common ingredient is a kind of invisibility. Sometimes the invisibility is real: The woman drops out of church. Other times the woman is present but remains unseen because she is different from the norm. Holidays such as Mother's Day can be extremely painful for women who want to be mothers but have been denied that role. An emphasis on the family can make single women feel invisible in a congregation. It's like being left-handed (which I am) in a right-handed world. Most people are right-handed, so why bother with things that make life a little easier for left-handed people? Most women are married (a view contrary to the statistics), so we lose sight of single women. Most married women are mothers, so we forget the pain experienced by infertile women or those who have lost children.

This chapter is about helping women love others as they love themselves, especially those who are different from themselves. Preachers must preach in such a way that all women are valued and seen as worthy of love and acceptance regardless of the particular roles they do or do not have. To love others, women must also see others. Preachers, therefore, must preach in such a way that all women are visible in the life of the church.

Stop ten people on the street and ask each one, "Who are you?" What kind of answers do you think you would get? It is likely that nine of the ten would describe themselves in terms of one or two of their most important roles. Most married women would probably define themselves by their relational roles: "I'm a wife and a mother." Single women and most men would more than likely define themselves by a professional role: "I'm a lawyer," or "I'm an accountant," or "I'm a plumber." Would such self-definitions really answer your question?

Now think about yourself. Take a moment to jot down at least fifteen roles you currently fill. You may have a wide range of relational roles that place demands on you throughout the year. If either of your parents is alive, you play a role as son or daughter, and if your grandparents or any aunts, uncles, or cousins are still living, you have obligations to them in your role as grandchild, nephew or niece, or cousin. If you are married, you play the role of a spouse, and if you are a parent, add the role you play in relation to your children. To your neighbors you are a neighbor. To your friends you are a friend (which may mean you are a mentor, a confidant, a tennis partner, and so on). After you have listed all your relational roles, list your professional roles. Add to them the roles you have in your community. By now you may have reached that minimum target of fifteen roles, or you may have gone well beyond that number.

We juggle a variety of roles every day. To keep from going crazy, we assign levels of importance to these roles: Some are primary, others are secondary, others are even lower. We emphasize some roles and ignore others in order to curb the demands they place on our limited time and energy. Social scientists call the act of ranking roles into a kind of hierarchy "role saliency." We make some roles salient, or important, and assign the rest to the fringes of our life. For some people, their most salient role becomes the way they define themselves. In fact, some people allow one role to engulf them so that they are never anything other than that role. For example, a professional person (a lawyer, a consultant, a doctor, a pastor) can be so engulfed in a professional role that even at home he or she plays that role with all its accoutrements—posture, tone of voice, or manner of speaking. Some of the problems encountered in families often have their roots in an engulfing role played by a parent who cannot leave the role at the office.

Marriages suffer when a wife and a husband place their marital roles at different levels of importance. Here is a helpful exercise: Ask couples to list their five or ten most important roles and to arrange them in a hierarchy of salience, putting the most important role at the top of the list. This can be an eye-opening exercise. When wives or husbands see how their spouses rate the marital role in relation to other roles, they may begin to see why they have felt neglected in the marriage.

In spite of the problems they pose, roles are necessary because they give structure to our lives. They organize our time and keep us productive. They also structure our expectations of others. I expect my husband to do certain things as my husband, and he expects certain things from me as his wife. For example, I expect him to keep the cars running and the house in repair, and he expects me to make dinner each evening. We expect each other to be faithful to our marriage vows, "to love and to cherish from this day forward, in sickness and in health, until death do us part." We made those promises to each other more than fifty years ago, and the expectation that each of us will keep those vows is part of how we define our marital roles.

But we are not the only ones who define our roles. Our social setting also defines roles for us. How my father loved my mother shaped my expectations of how my husband should love me. How his mother loved his father shaped his expectations of me. Furthermore, both of us were shaped by the cultural attitudes present at the time we married each other (in 1951). Roles are developed internally, but there are often unspoken but powerful external pressures at work.

What happens when a central role (one we put at the top of our list) is lost? Much pastoral counseling focuses on helping people through the trauma of losing an important role. A wife or husband loses the marital role through divorce or the death of a spouse. A worker loses a professional role when a company downsizes and lays off much of its staff. A parent grieves the loss of a child—and the loss of the role as parent to that child. The loss of a salient role brings not only grief but major readjustments to life.

Roles shift and change over time. No role remains the same throughout a lifetime. Children grow up, changing the parent role. People age and retire from jobs, removing a professional role. Death invades life again and again, and roles change. It is obvious, therefore, that identity is not synonymous with roles. *Identity* is "who we are," whereas a *role* is "what we do." Roles tell us what we may expect people to do, but they do not tell us who those people *are*. We must look beyond roles to understand personhood or identity.

Whenever we confuse roles with identity, we imprison people in roles that represent only a small part of who God made them to be. For women to love themselves and others, they must realize that who they are is not the same as what they do.

Women and Role Expectations

Can a woman be fully a woman if she does not have the roles of wife and mother?[1] It is possible that single women or married women without children are given reasons in church to believe that only wives who are mothers are truly "women." Preachers can convey unintended messages to single or childless women that they are less than complete in their personhood. For example, sermons on holidays such as Mother's Day can support the assumption that all adult women are married or will be, and all married women are mothers or will be. Just as a professional role is not the complete identity of a man, neither is a marital role the complete identity of a woman. Yet for many single or infertile women, the message they hear may imply that they cannot be "true" women until they marry and bear a child.

Ministering to the Single Woman

The first step in ministering to single women is to understand how many of them there are. Albert Hsu (writing in 1997) reported that

> throughout the nineteenth and the first half of the twentieth century, less than 5 percent of the U.S. adult population was single. However, in the last thirty years the percentage of singles has increased dramatically. In 1996 the U.S. Census Bureau reported that 43 percent of U.S. adults were single: either never married, widowed, or divorced. Another 3.5 percent were legally married but separated from their spouses. The remaining 53.5 percent of adults were married and had their spouses present. Some experts predict that single adults will account for fully half of the adult population by the turn of the century.[2]

Women are waiting longer to get married: First-time brides are older today than at any other time in the past one hundred years. Fewer people are getting married: Between 1960 and 2000, the percentage of all persons age 15 and older who were married dropped for men from 69.3 percent to 57.9 percent, and for women from 65.9 percent to 54.2 percent. This means that in the year 2000, 45.8 percent of all women age 15 and older were single. Before dismissing that statistic because it includes teenage young women, note that of all women age 35 to 44 (according to the 1999 U.S. Bureau of Census), only 71.2 percent were married, with 28.8 percent single in the "most married" years of people's lives. Many singles fear divorce: They are the sons and daughters of the most-divorced generation in American history and do not want to repeat the mistakes of their parents.[3] We will not minister effectively to single women if we do not take the sheer number of them seriously.

Second, to minister effectively to single women, thereby helping them to love themselves and others, we must know the messages that singles receive from both the culture and the church that distort their personhood. Though recent television series such as *Judging Amy* have helped to create more open and accepting attitudes toward singles in the wider culture, the perception of singleness is still negative. Social psychologists may refer to singles as "those who fail to marry" or "those who do not make positive choices." Single women are often puzzles to their married friends and relatives, and they are asked bold questions: "Do you have a boyfriend?" "You're a nice girl. Why aren't you dating anyone?" Or "So, you're still single?" Often these well-intentioned friends or relatives assure single women that "God has someone very special for you." Or "You'll make someone a perfect wife!" Or "I hope you'll meet someone special—I really want you to be happy." Singles are made to feel that marriage is the only natural arrangement, and those who do not think so are odd, strange, or deviant.[4]

Within the church, singles are often grouped together solely on the basis of their marital status, not on any similarity of interests or needs. Hsu illustrates this with Walter, twenty-four years old, who said, "My pastor is always trying to match me up with someone else in the church, even if she's thirty-three years old and not my type."[5] The common assumption in many singles ministries is that all single women are interested in finding a mate. In the church, singleness is seen as something to get out of, something to fear, something to pray that you never have to experience. There is little understanding or acceptance of the notion that both marriage and singleness are gifts from God and that both can be fully embraced.

Third, to minister effectively to single women, we must examine our own attitudes toward singleness and marriage and the way they influence our ministry. Hsu reports that though singles comprise nearly half of the adult population in the United States, singles comprise only 15 percent of the adults in most churches. The smaller the church, the lower the percentage of singles.[6] Mary Stewart Van Leeuwen notes that "despite the fact that Christians pay lip service to the equal value of married and single people, their near-idolatry of the family over the past century has made single Christians feel like second-class citizens at best and moral failures at worst."[7] While the wider culture has made a shift toward validating single women, church programs continue to be oriented mostly toward traditional families.

This inflicts severe pain on single women. Over the years many such women have talked to me about their marginalization in the church:

They are not considered "adults" until they are married. They are called "girls" until they wed, notwithstanding their professional achievement or their spiritual maturity. Single women sense others' assumption that being married is the only "right" and "godly" goal they should have. This, of course, flies in the face of the apostle Paul's teaching in 1 Corinthians 7 as well as the example of his own life. Yet it is difficult for single women to feel valued until they have been chosen by a man for matrimony. The pressure to conform drives them to singles "meat markets" and at times even into depression. Many leave the church or move from church to church, hoping to find a place where singleness is not seen as a disease.

If we believe that a woman is not fully a woman until she is a wife, a single woman in the church will never be validated as a whole person. In many cases, this means a denial of her spiritual gifts. Yet single Christian women, as much as anyone else in the congregation, have a strong need to use their gifts in ministry. They must understand their identity as Christians and see how they fit into the body of Christ. Douglas Fagerstrom noted that

> the lack of a family is not going to keep a single woman from a promotion in her profession. When the church offers few opportunities for women to be involved, it is not uncommon for the career-oriented single woman to seek that feeling of significance and value in the workplace rather than the church.[8]

Single women need opportunities to contribute meaningful work to the kingdom of God, work that uses their God-given gifts and abilities. The apostle Paul makes it clear that gifts are given to the church for the benefit of all its members. When the gifts of single women lie dormant, the entire church suffers.

Singleness is merely a role, not a core identity. Single women need a sense of community in a church that is welcoming, comfortable, and safe, a church in which married people and singles blend together in fellowship and ministry. A congregation can lay the groundwork for such relationships if the vision for such relationships is present.[9]

Singles are full persons and have much to contribute to a congregation. Preachers need to reinforce this view so that single women can love themselves and others and so that those who are married can love those who are not.

Ministering to the Infertile Woman

If typical Mother's Day sermons make single women feel uncomfortable, this is even more true for married women who have not been able to give birth. When a married woman who is eager to start a family discovers that getting pregnant is not easy for her, she may initially think, "We didn't time it right" or "There's still next month." But as the months turn into years, the questions mount, and with the questions come feelings of anger, frustration, and sorrow. This woman-without-a-child is on an emotional roller coaster, zooming up with hope each month, then dropping sharply down as another menstrual period begins and hope is dashed.[10] Every day she is confronted with reminders of her childlessness—children at play on the sidewalk, baby showers for friends, diapers in the supermarket aisle, and the rounded bellies of pregnant women at church or at the mall. Add to those reminders the insensitive remarks about her childlessness, family pressures, and possibly even a marriage crisis. Threaded through all these events is the never-ending yearning for a child.[11]

Infertility is a physiological condition, but it comes with enormous emotional and spiritual freight for the husband and wife who desperately want a child of their own. It is estimated that one out of every six couples of childbearing age has fertility problems,[12] with more than six million people in the United States currently dealing with infertility.[13] Although infertility is typically considered a woman's problem, statistics point to an even division of the problem between men and women: In one-third of the cases, only the wife is infertile; in one-third of the cases, only the husband is infertile; in one-third of the cases, infertility is present in both the husband and the wife.[14] Roughly 95 percent of infertile people are infertile because of diagnosable medical problems, and slightly more than half of these people can eventually have a baby with proper medical diagnosis and treatment.[15]

But what about those who cannot have a child of their own? Month after month as they ricochet between hope and despair, the cycle drains them emotionally. Once they have accepted the reality that they cannot have a child, they grieve what will never be. Some therapists treat infertility as a chronic illness because often there is no final resolution as with a clear-cut loss.[16] This lack of resolution places added strain on a marriage. When either partner is the sole cause of the infertility, he or she may struggle with feelings of failure, guilt, shame, self-pity, and fear that the spouse will leave the marriage.[17] Every couple also struggles with the stress of uncertainty (will a pregnancy eventually come?) and finds it difficult to move ahead with life. Some choose to adopt (not an easy process in most cases). Others accept the painful reality that they will lead a child-free life.

Infertility for Christian couples frequently brings a spiritual crisis as well, as they wonder why God is deliberately withholding a child from them. It is not unusual for such couples to doubt God's goodness, his faithfulness, even his existence. Some women and men scrutinize the past, looking for a sin for which infertility is a punishment. Others believe they are not good enough to be parents and thus have been denied the opportunity. They try to discern whether God is trying to teach them something through the experience. Underlying all their questions is the basic question of theodicy: Why does God allow bad things to happen to good people? As couples struggle with that question, they also struggle with whether God is good and whether they can trust him.

Women receive a cultural message that being a mother is the center of their identity. Sandra Glahn and William Cutrer state, "American women grow up thinking of motherhood as a central—if not *the* central—role in their lives. While many men also want to become parents, theirs is no 'fatherhood mandate' with the same force and intensity as the 'motherhood mandate.'"[18] This "motherhood mandate" exists for women from early childhood throughout adulthood. The view that they need to become a mother is ingrained in them, and when this expectation is not fulfilled because of infertility, their identity as a woman shatters. When women allow culture to define who they are, those who are infertile may live their lives with a sense of incompleteness.

Unfortunately, many women receive the same "motherhood mandate" message in church. Being a mother is presented not only as the central role and identity for a woman but also as her highest calling.[19] In churches in which women are taught that the chief end of marriage is to have children, infertile women struggle with the meaning of their marriages. But Scripture does not teach that motherhood is the highest calling for a woman,[20] and when churches teach that it is (explicitly or implicitly), infertile women experience great mental and emotional strain. Even if not taught formally by a church, the same message is often conveyed by special events that glorify motherhood or by insensitive comments to childless couples.

Motherhood is a role, not an identity. It is not the entirety of a woman's life, nor is it the mark of her identity as a woman. Preachers can offer women, single or married, with children or without, the liberating possibility of finding their true identity in Christ.

How Does This Apply to Preaching?

The apostle Paul was explicit about the benefits of the single life:

> I wish that all men were even as I myself. But each one has his own gift from God, one in this manner and another in that. But I say to the unmarried and to the widows: It is good for them if they remain even as I am; but if they cannot exercise self-control, let them marry. For it is better to marry than to burn with passion. . . . I want you to be without care. He who is unmarried cares for the things that belong to the Lord—how he may please the Lord. But he who is married cares about the things of the world—how he may please his wife. There is a difference between a wife and a virgin. The unmarried woman cares about the things of the Lord, that she may be holy both in body and in spirit. But she who is married cares about the things of the world—how she may please her husband. And this I say for your own profit, not that I may put a leash on you, but for what is proper, and that you may serve the Lord without distraction. . . . A wife is bound by law as long as her husband lives; but if her husband dies, she is at liberty to be married to whom she wishes, only in the Lord. But she is happier if she remains as she is, according to my judgment—and I think I also have the Spirit of God.
>
> 1 Corinthians 7:7–9, 32–35, 39–40

According to the apostle Paul, marriage complicates service to Christ because it can divide allegiances to God and one's spouse. Marriage can sidetrack Christians from serving God. Mary Stewart Van Leeuwen captured the sense of this passage:

> We should . . . note that by restoring the family to its secondary biblical place we can come a long way toward recovering a biblical respect for singleness. . . . When both states (marriage and singleness) are evaluated in kingdom terms, their functions are clearly complementary: a stable Christian family may have a missionary advantage in providing hospitality. But the single person, unencumbered with family duties, often has the missionary advantage of mobility. And both are vital to the spread of the Church.[21]

Thus, ministering to the whole church means preaching the complementarity of single persons and married persons. This is an essential part of preaching the whole counsel of God, which validates every member of the body, single or married.

Second, every Christian must know that his or her identity is in Jesus Christ, not in roles that come and go. Who we are is bound up not merely in what we *do* but in who we *are* as the unique work of God's hands. We are made in God's image, and while theologians disagree about the fine points implied in that statement, it suggests many ways in which our identity is manifested: in the minds God gave us, in the aesthetic sense God placed within us, and in the power to choose good over evil. Most of all, it implies a spiritual nature that opens us to a relationship with the One whose image we bear in this world. Both men and women need to hear about the God whose image we carry throughout a lifetime and for eternity. This identity transcends whatever roles we play in this life.

God, speaking through the prophet Isaiah, gave comfort to those who were childless:

> "Sing, O barren woman,
>   you who never bore a child;
> burst into song, shout for joy,
>   you who were never in labor;
> because more are the children of the desolate woman
>   than of her who has a husband," says the LORD. . . .
> Let not any eunuch complain,
>   "I am only a dry tree."
> For this is what the LORD says:
> "To the eunuchs who keep my Sabbaths,
>   who choose what pleases me
>   and hold fast to my covenant—
> to them I will give within my temple and its walls
>   a memorial and a name
>   better than sons and daughters;
> I will give them an everlasting name
>   that will not be cut off."
>
> Isaiah 54:1; 56:3–5 NIV

That is God's vision for those who may feel they are less than whole persons because of singleness or barrenness. Preaching to encourage these members of the body of Christ requires understanding the messages these women receive, both from the culture and from the church. It may require rethinking your own assumptions about singleness or infertility. It will require probing the Word of God for messages that speak against the idolatry of the family. The Bible provides probable examples of single women and infertile women. Miriam, one of the three leaders of Israel (Micah 6:4) in the exodus from Egypt, was most likely a single woman, as were several of the women who worked alongside Paul—Phoebe (Rom. 16:1–2), Mary (Rom. 16:6), Tryphena, Tryphosa, and Persis (Rom. 16:12), as well as Euodia and Syntyche (Phil. 4:2). Some barren women in the Scriptures eventually had a child (Sarah in Genesis 21, Rachel in Genesis 30, Hannah in 1 Samuel 1–2, Elizabeth in Luke 1), but not every married lover of God had a child. Though she was married seven years, the widowed prophetess Anna most likely remained childless (Luke 2). While we cannot be certain about the marital status of these women or whether they had children, one thing is clear: They were not defined in Scripture by a role of wife or mother.

It is possible for single women and childless women to bring many sons and daughters into God's kingdom. Preach to encourage them in the state to which they are called. Do not confuse passing roles with permanent identities. Hold God's Word out to them as an anchor for their hearts, souls, minds, and strength. Only then will they be able to love themselves and others.

Preach also to the married with children to embrace those who are not called to that state. Encourage them to share their lives and love with women who are different from them. Part of preaching the Great Commandment is being specific about what it means to love one's neighbor as oneself. When the Jewish lawyer asked Jesus to define *neighbor* (Luke 10:29), he hoped for a narrow definition that would rule out people unlike himself. But Jesus turned his view upside down with the parable of the Good Samaritan. Your neighbor may well be unlike you. Your neighbor may even be a sworn enemy. Your neighbor is anyone whose need you see, whose need you are able to meet.[22] Neighbor-love is integral to the Great Commandment and integral to life in the church. Preach the interdependency of the body. Give those who are married and those with children reasons to reach out to singles in the congregation and to those with empty arms. If you do, you will enable your listeners to fulfill the last part of the Great Commandment.[23]

Summing Up the Chapter

- Roles are necessary because they give structure to our lives. They organize our time and keep us productive. They also structure our expectations of one another.
- Roles tell us what we may expect people to do, but they do not tell us who those people *are*. We must look beyond roles to understand personhood or identity.
- Preachers can convey unintended messages to women that they are less than complete in their personhood because they are either not married or not mothers.
- To minister effectively to single women, we must examine our own attitudes toward singleness and marriage and the way they influence our ministry.
- Single women need a sense of community in a church that is welcoming, comfortable, and safe, a church in which married people and singles blend together in fellowship and ministry.
- Infertility for Christian couples frequently brings a spiritual crisis as they wonder why God is deliberately withholding a child from them.
- Women receive a cultural message that being a mother is the center of their identity.
- Motherhood is a role, not an identity. It is not the entirety of a woman's life, nor is it the mark of her identity as a woman.
- Marriage complicates service to Christ and can sidetrack Christians from serving God.
- A stable Christian family may have a missionary advantage in providing hospitality, but a single person, unencumbered with family duties, often has the advantage of mobility. Both are vital to missions.
- It is possible for single women and childless women to bring many sons and daughters into God's kingdom. Preach to encourage them in the state to which they are called.
- Give those who are married and those with children reasons to reach out to singles in the congregation and to those with empty arms.

Questions to Ponder

- Think about your congregation: Which groups within the church may be "invisible" because they are different from the majority of the members? How can you preach to make visible those who are invisible? What difference do you think that would make in your church?
- Examine your own feelings and beliefs about singleness: How do your feelings and beliefs affect how you preach to single women in your congregation?
- What are your social or role expectations for women in the church? Do these expectations cut you off from any groups of women in the congregation?
- How can you preach the Great Commandment so that women will embrace and include those who are different from themselves?

10

Understanding Women as Listeners

In Neil Simon's play *Jake's Women,* Jake is a best-selling author who constantly carries on imaginary conversations with six women in his life: his sister, his deceased first wife, his estranged second wife, his daughter, his shrink, and his current paramour. Jake conjures up these women for the audience, and we hear the conversations as though the women were actually present. To the women, however, the conversations are frustrating because Jake consistently puts *his* words into their mouths. Finally, in a real conversation with his estranged wife, he is forced to see that she has her own thoughts, which are very different from those he imputes to her in his imaginary conversations. In a heated argument with Jake, she shouts words to this effect: "You have never really listened to me! You don't have a clue about my point of view!" In the end, Jake acknowledges her reality and begins the difficult task of setting aside his authorial stance and trying to see things from her point of view.

This book has attempted to exegete a sometimes alien point of view. Point of view is important in preaching. It is the stance, or position in time and space, taken by a speaker. It includes the attitudes and values that surface in a sermon. How a preacher feels about non-Christians, economic issues, or people of a different race or social status comes through (consciously or otherwise) in the metaphors and illustrations used in a message. That also holds true for a minister's attitudes toward women. How can preachers analyze their stance toward women as they preach each week? Following are six questions[1] that may help preachers relate to women in their congregations so as to help them realize that the Good News is for them.

Do We Typecast Men and Women in Traditional Stereotyped Roles?

Most actors resent being typecast. Rather than always playing the same kind of character, they prefer a broad scope for their acting talents. As men and women juggle their multiple roles (discussed in chap. 9), they too want the freedom to express their gifts and abilities in various ways. Yet it is easy to pigeonhole men and women in stereotyped roles.

When a man joins our church, do we immediately measure him for some kind of leadership role? Do we also wonder if his wife would be a good addition to the hospitality committee? Some men will never be leaders, and some women do not find cookie-baking or table-decorating fulfilling. This kind of typecasting easily spills over into preaching, showing up in the examples we choose to illustrate our points.

Typecasting also overrides both gifts and calling, hurting not only the women in our congregations but the church at large. David Neff pointed to typecasting in a *Christianity Today* editorial (chap. 3) as a possible reason for the 40 percent difference in self-esteem between men and women entering a Bible college to prepare for Christian service. The illustrations we choose often subtly reinforce this typecasting.

Do We Represent Both Men and Women as Whole Human Beings?

Do we allow men to be emotional? Do we let women act independently? Do we praise men when they are gentle? Do we value a woman's directness when she speaks out? Do we truly believe a woman has the capacity to be logical? Or that a man has the capacity to be neat?[2]

If we find ourselves praising a certain characteristic in a man but looking down on that same characteristic in a woman, we have probably fallen into a form of stereotyping. We can sensitize people in our congregation to these issues by choosing women as examples of active accomplishment or using men as examples of quiet passivity or fearful indecision. All of us are whole human beings, and none of us—men or women—should be cut off from part of our humanity because of a stereotype.

Do We Accord Men and Women the Same Level of Respect?

There are many ways in which we may unconsciously show one half of the human race less respect than we show the other. For example, some people describe women by their physical attributes or their marital status, while they describe men by their intellectual capacity or their occupation. Sometimes media commentators focus on the content of a male politician's speech but report on a female politician's appearance rather than the content of what she says.

Another form of disrespect involves sexual innuendos, describing women as sex objects or as weak and helpless, or referring to women with terms such as "the weaker sex," "a woman's libber," or "girl." The words *boy* and *girl* look symmetrical, but we do not always use them symmetrically. We would seldom call an adult male in our congregation a boy because we recognize that he is an adult: He is a *man*. After all, he holds down a job and supports himself. Yet in our culture, *girl* is used to describe females of all ages, including adult women who hold down jobs and support themselves. Why the one and not the other? Calling a man a boy belittles his experience, his competence, his adult attributes. In the same way, calling a woman a girl reduces her to the status of a dependent child.

Virginia Sapiro reminds us that for decades the word *boy* was used by some whites in regard to African American men. To call an African American *boy* was to put him in his place. It stripped him of his manhood. Abolishing the use of that term was an important symbolic issue during the civil rights movement of the 1950s and 1960s. Within a generation that usage has virtually disappeared, but the parallel use of *girl* for an adult woman has not.[3] Unconsciously, our words may say what we do not mean and convey a lack of respect.

Do We Recognize Both Men and Women for Their Own Achievements?

Prior to the Industrial Revolution, men and women worked side by side for the sustenance of their families. Historians tell us about women carrying on family trades long after their husbands' deaths because the two had worked together in smithing or weaving or candle-making. Yet women have been told from many pulpits that their greatest achievement lies in giving loving support to a husband who achieves for them. Many of the problems of self-esteem and depression with which women struggle can be traced directly to the assumption that women do not merit their own place in the sun. This attitude affects single women as well as married women and denigrates their dreams and accomplishments.

Does Our Language Exclude Women When We Talk about Humanity as a Whole?

Words are the tools we use to express our thoughts, feelings, and desires to other people. Individual words can have a wide range of connotations or implied meanings. Our words may reflect our unconscious attitudes about gender.

Here are five practices that can go a long way toward sensitizing others to gender issues.

First, when referring to a group that includes women, avoid using "man" as a generic term. Today, not everyone hears it as generic. Instead, substitute "people" or "persons" or "humanity" or "men and women." The New Testament writers were careful to distinguish between *anēr* and *anthropos* when writing about a male person *(anēr)* or about humanity in general *(anthropos)*. Translators have been less careful and have translated both Greek words into the English word *man*. We ought to reflect the original biblical care by including women intentionally when we refer to a mixed group.

Second, when referring to people in general, avoid using "he," "him," and "his." Change the sentence slightly to make it universal. For example, instead of saying, "The average American drinks his coffee black," simply drop the pronoun *his:* "The average American drinks coffee black." Or stay with the third person but make the sentence plural: "Most Americans drink their coffee black." It is a simple shift, but it includes both halves of the human race.

Third, give some attention to occupational terms that have changed over the years. A preacher who still refers to a flight attendant as a stewardess ignores the fact that many men now serve the public on commercial airlines. The devastation of September 11 at the World Trade Center and the Pentagon reminded all of us that both men and women fight fires and risk their lives to save lives. Thus, we now speak of fire fighters and police officers, not firemen or policemen.

Fourth, avoid language that assumes listeners are male. Preachers who refer to "you and your wife" while speaking to a mixed audience betray the "true" audience being addressed. It is better to refer to "you and your spouse," which includes women in the audience.

Finally, when appropriate, emphasize that a passage applies to women as well as to men. Years ago at a women's retreat, the speaker read 2 Corinthians 5:17. But she made one daring change in the text. She said, "If anyone is in Christ, *she* is a new creation; old things have passed away; behold, all things have become new." Suddenly, that passage gripped me in a new way. I realized that tears were trickling down my face and that I was trying to swallow a lump in my throat. I had read or quoted that verse scores of times over the years, but for the first time it felt truly personal to me. If you had asked me earlier if Paul had addressed those words to women as well as to men, I would have assured you that he had. Intellectually, I knew the verse included me. But that day at the women's retreat, I discovered *emotionally* that the verse included me.

We must not be careless in handling the Word of God. But there are times when we read Scripture in public that we can unleash the power of the Word in women's lives simply by reading the text as it appears in our translation and then rereading the text with female pronouns. This is particularly appropriate when the text is not gender-specific in the original language (as is true of 2 Cor. 5:17).

Do We Use Language That Designates and Describes Men and Women on Equal Terms?

If the minister at the end of a wedding ceremony were to say, "I now pronounce you *husband and woman*," what message would that convey? In such a case, the man would be designated by his role, husband, but the woman would be accorded her full personhood. When the minister says, "I now pronounce you *man and wife*," the woman is reduced to a single role while the man is given full personhood. Because a marriage ceremony joins a man and a woman as husband and wife, it is better to use the correlating terms: "I now pronounce you *husband and wife*."

Reversing gender in common expressions can help people develop sensitivity to gender issues. If these reverse statements strike us as absurd or demeaning to men, then the original expressions may well be absurd or demeaning in regard to women.

Understanding Women as Listeners

Back in 1993, William Hendricks published a series of exit interviews with men and women who had decided to leave the churches they had attended. He summarized a part of his findings with these words:

> If some of the comments from the women I spoke with are any indication, the church has a time bomb on its hands. Women are angry and getting angrier. I would not presume to characterize all women in the church this way. But the message is loud and clear: when it comes to issues like language, opportunities, praise and rewards, authority, staffing, expectations, marriage and sexuality, and justice, women increasingly see the church as dominated by a male perspective. Many feel that Christianity as represented by its institutions and leaders comes across as insensitive. Certainly they would say there are exceptions, but overall it feels like a system that does not respect women.[4]

These are words we would rather not hear. But Hendricks is not alone in observing the ongoing exodus of women from Christian churches. In more than three decades of ministry to women, I have listened again and again to the heartbreak of women who wanted to love God with all their hearts, souls, minds, and strength but who could not hear or see a biblical vision of God in the church.

Hendricks reported his interview with one woman whose search for God (after disappointment in various churches) took her to a conservative evangelical seminary in the Southwest. She talked about her classes and a woman classmate in these words:

> I remember a woman from England who didn't care either way for this issue of what women can or can't do in the church. That wasn't an issue for her. But she began getting really angry in one class we both had because, as she said, "the image of God

> was being abused in her soul." I thought that was so articulate, because God made male and female, and the professor was so restrictive with the female role that it tightened my chest almost. . . . Being a man, I don't know that you'll ever quite know how that feels.

Hendricks concluded his assessment of the interview as follows:

> Much of Deana's frustration at this period, both at seminary and at most of the churches she tried, was that she wasn't feeling respected as a woman and as a person. She didn't feel that her emotions mattered, that her doubts mattered, or that any alternative points of view might be considered as having anything to offer. Things were just a little bit too neatly buttoned down to be realistic.[5]

My hope is that this book will help you preach so that all the "Deanas" in your congregation can hear clearly the Good News of God's grace and love and can learn to love God with all their hearts, souls, minds, and strength, and their neighbor as themselves. That goes to the heart of what preaching is about. When you enable your listeners to love God and others with every part of their being, you have done a great work for them and for God's kingdom.

Questions to Ponder

- Suppose 60 percent of your congregation were under the age of twenty-five. Would that affect the way you preach? If 60 percent (or more) of your congregation were made up of women, how would this fact affect your preaching?
- When women speak (in meetings, Bible study groups, or personal conversation), do you really listen to them? Do you ask questions so that you can understand what they are saying and why?
- If you use illustrations about athletes, surgeons, executives, pilots, or leaders, do you make many of them women?
- Do you make it a point to convey that the skills of homemakers are as important as skills in the workplace? Do you commend the gifts of single women as much as you laud the married state and motherhood?
- Do you preach sermons during the year that feature strong women of the Bible? What about a series on these women?[6]

- When you preach from narrative sections of the Bible, do you ever look at the stories from the perspectives of the women involved?
- As you lead your congregation in prayer and pray for those who are hurting, do you ever pray for those in the church who are in abusive marriages or for children who are being sexually abused?
- Do you apply biblical principles to life situations where they can be used? Do your applications reflect the complex situations in which faith must be practiced?
- Do you ever indulge in humor that demeans people of the opposite sex? Why?
- If you are male and married, do you ask your wife to help you make your sermons relevant to women? Would you be willing to ask half a dozen women in your congregation to critique your sermons for gender concerns?

Notes

Chapter 1

1. This exercise was first published in Virginia Sapiro, *Women in American Society* (Palo Alto, Calif.: Mayfield Publishing, 1986), 255.

2. As a follow-up to this exercise, you may want to jot down some notes about your adult life as it is today. How much of what you do or don't do is determined by gender?

3. While women who teach or preach may also read this book, the vast majority of preachers in pulpits today are men, for many of whom the "female experience of life" may be opaque.

4. Frederick Buechner, *Telling the Truth* (San Francisco: Harper & Row, 1977), 22–23.

5. Roy McCloughry, *Men and Masculinity: From Power to Love* (London: Hodder & Stoughton, 1992), 208.

6. Deborah Tannen, *You Just Don't Understand: Men and Women in Conversation* (London: Virago, 1991), quoted in ibid., 210.

7. For an excellent extended discussion of culturally relevant ministry, see Paul Hiebert, *Anthropological Insights for Missionaries* (Grand Rapids: Baker, 1985).

8. Elizabeth Aries raises important questions about this "two-culture" approach to gender, noting that it fails to recognize the importance of sexual inequalities at a societal level. I have chosen to acknowledge her concern for power inequalities between men and women but not to make that a part of this book. For her discussion of this issue, see Elizabeth Aries, *Men and Women in Interaction: Reconsidering the Differences* (New York: Oxford University Press, 1996), 195ff.

9. Ann Firor Scott, "On Seeing and Not Seeing: A Case of Historical Invisibility," *The Journal of American History* 71, no. 1 (1984): 7, 19.

10. This is not the same use of the word *knowledge* as that of philosophers.

11. This is not to say that gender explains all the difference between my husband and me! We were both shaped by our families of origin and by our diverse experiences as adults in our social context.

12. In Greek literature, the Hydra was a mythical monster with nine heads. As Hercules attempted to slay this beast by lopping off a head, two heads would grow in its place unless the wound was immediately cauterized. The Hydra came to symbolize any multifarious evil, according to *Webster's Collegiate Dictionary,* 2d ed. (Springfield, Mass.: G & C Merriam Co., 1949).

13. Studies of ethnic prejudice have clearly identified the strong tendency for "difference" to become the basis for discrimination against the one who is different.

14. Gilbert Keith Chesterton, *Orthodoxy* (New York: John Lane, 1909).

15. There are some strange bedfellows in the gender wars. Many conservative Christians and some radical feminists (such as Dr. Mary Daly) both tend to exaggerate the difference between men and women.

16. Anne Fausto-Sterling, *Myths of Gender: Biological Theories about Women and Men* (New York: Basic Books, 1985), 34–36.

17. MOPS is the acronym for a Colorado-based national parachurch ministry, Mothers of Preschoolers.

18. Cited in J. Williams, *Psychology of Women: Behavior in a Biosocial Context,* 3d ed. (New York: W. W. Norton, 1987), 97.

19. For example, see Elisabeth Elliot, "The Essence of Femininity: A Personal Perspective," chapter 25 in John Piper and Wayne Grudem, *Recovering Biblical Manhood and Womanhood* (Wheaton: Crossway, 1991), 397.

20. More dangerous is that such teaching opens the door to a sociobiological view of gender differences that sees such differences as biological and thus irreversible. This creates the possibility of a victim mentality: One can argue that he or she bears no responsibility for outcomes that are the result of something "biological." A rapist actually pled "not guilty" in a court of law on the basis that he was a victim of his testosterone. God holds us responsible for our actions, which a victimization theory of gender would not allow. If, on the other hand, differences between men and women stem from an interaction between our sex and our gender (learning), we can evaluate which of them might be immutable and which may need to be changed.

Chapter 2

1. *The Interpreter's Dictionary of the Bible,* vol. 2 (New York: Abingdon Press, 1962), 549–50.

2. This includes not only the Ten Commandments but all the biblical teachings governing our moral decision-making.

3. Lawrence Kohlberg, "The Development of Children's Orientation toward a Moral Order: I. Sequences in the Development of Human Thought," *Vita Humana* 6 (1963): 11–33. For those who wish to read more about Kohlberg's work, see L. Kohlberg, *The Philosophy of Moral Development: Moral Stages and the Idea of Justice: Essays on Moral Development,* vol. 1 (San Francisco: Harper & Row, 1982); and L. Kohlberg, *The Psychology of Moral Development: Moral Stages and the Idea of Justice: Essays on Moral Development,* vol. 2 (San Francisco: Harper & Row, 1984).

4. In the first stage, a young child obeys the rules to avoid punishment, and in the second stage, he or she obeys the rules to get rewards. In both cases, the decision to be obedient is based on the child's concern for self and survival. At some point, school-age children begin to conform to the rules, not for tangible rewards but for the approval of other people (stage 3): They become "good" boys or "good" girls. Some then go on to stage 4, in which they develop a law-and-order way of thinking. They do not want to be censured for breaking rules, so they develop a rigid conformity to the rules. In stages 3 and 4, people develop a concern for others and their opinions. They want to live in a way that is responsible to the needs of others in society. Stage-5 people still obey the rules because they make it possible for people to live together peacefully, but they see the rules as being flexible. Stage-6 people develop internal principles (such as justice or equality) by which they live in order to avoid self-condemnation. Both stage-5 and stage-6 people may violate society's rules if they believe the rules infringe on the interdependence they share with people around them. For

a helpful chart and some further discussion of Kohlberg's schema, see Janet Shibley Hyde, *Half the Human Experience: The Psychology of Women*, 4th ed. (Lexington, Mass.: D. C. Heath, 1991), 49–52.

5. Ibid., 51.

6. Carol Gilligan, *In a Different Voice* (Cambridge: Harvard University Press, 1982), 18.

7. M. Gay Hubbard has observed that "such inappropriate generalization might be viewed simply as unfortunate if it were not for the amount of unquestioning acceptance that greeted Kohlberg's work and the presumed evidence it provided for the woman-as-deficient school of thought" (M. Gay Hubbard, *Women: The Misunderstood Majority* [Waco: Word, 1992], 149).

8. Gilligan, *In a Different Voice,* 16.

9. Frederica Mathewes-Green, *Real Choices: Listening to Women; Looking for Alternatives to Abortion* (Ben Lomond, Calif.: Conciliar Press, 1994, 1997).

10. Measured on Kohlberg's scale, some of the parental concerns and the boyfriends' concerns would turn out to be stage-1 decisions made on the basis of concern for themselves.

11. Participants in this study were in the sixth grade and participated in the rights and responsibilities study to explore different conceptions of morality and self. Gilligan, *In a Different Voice,* 25.

12. This sets up a hierarchy of competing principles. An extended explication of this approach to moral decision-making is found in Norman Geisler, *Ethics: Alternatives and Issues* (Grand Rapids: Zondervan, 1971), in which the author hierarchizes a series of biblically derived principles for moral decision-making so that "competing" principles are no longer coordinate but one is subordinate to the other. In Geisler's schema, the hierarchy of principles eliminates the problem of deciding between principles.

13. Writing from a Christian perspective, I want to state clearly that neither Kohlberg nor Gilligan deals with morality from a specifically biblical perspective. When Kohlberg holds that people in stage 6 operate on "internal principles," these principles do not necessarily overlap with what Christian ethicists would consider to be universal principles of morality. In Kohlberg's view, whatever principles a person has internalized give that individual the right to abrogate laws or rules that impede a particular decision. For example, an internalized principle of justice could theoretically lead to acts of retaliatory violence as in clan warfare.

14. Gilligan, *In a Different Voice,* 29.

15. Ibid., 31.

16. Ibid., 164.

17. Carol Gilligan, "Moral Orientation and Moral Development," in *Women and Moral Theory,* ed. Eva Feder Kittay and Diana T. Meyers (Totowa, N.J.: Rowman & Littlefield, 1987), 19–20.

18. Gilligan's conclusions came out of her discussion of the work of Nancy Chodorow in *The Reproduction of Mothering* (Berkeley: University of California Press, 1978).

19. Gilligan, *In a Different Voice,* 8.

20. Thus, Gilligan writes, "For boys and men, separation and individuation are critically tied to gender identity since separation from the mother is essential for the development of masculinity. For girls and women, issues of femininity or feminine identity do not depend on the achievement of separation from the mother or on the progress of individuation. Since masculinity is defined through separation while femininity is defined through attachment, male gender identity is threatened by intimacy while female gender identity is threatened by separation. Thus males tend to have difficulty with relationships, while females tend to have problems with individuation. The quality of embeddedness in social interaction and personal relationships that characterizes women's lives in contrast to men's, however, becomes not only a descriptive difference but also a developmental liability. . . . Women's failure to separate then becomes by definition a failure to develop" (ibid., 8–9).

21. Janet Lever, "Sex Differences in the Games Children Play," *Social Problems* 23 (1976): 478–87, cited in Gilligan, *In a Different Voice,* 9. While I first noted the connection between the observa-

tions of Lever, Piaget, Miller, and Woolf while reading Gilligan, I am citing the original sources so that a reader interested in pursuing their ideas can more easily locate them.

22. Jean Piaget, *The Moral Judgment of the Child* (1932; reprint, New York: Free Press, 1965), 83.

23. Ibid., 77.

24. Jean Baker Miller, *Toward a New Psychology of Women* (Boston: Beacon Press, 1976), 83.

25. Virginia Woolf, *A Room of One's Own* (New York: Harcourt, Brace & World, 1929), 76.

26. The illustration of a pregnant teenager at the beginning of the chapter illustrates this: Should concern for the opinions, desires, or commands of her parents or boyfriend decide the issue, or should the unborn child's right to life be the primary concern in weighing competing rights? The competition between or among rights may be between persons (as in the case of the influential people in the pregnant teenager's life) or between rules, laws, or principles (as in the conflict between the right to life and the right to reproductive freedom).

27. Many women, in fact, believe that any success they may have will always be at someone else's expense. This is discussed in greater detail in chapter 4.

28. Cindy Simon Rosenthal, *When Women Lead: Integrative Leadership in State Legislatures* (New York: Oxford University Press, 1998).

29. For an extended discussion of this, see Sally Helgesen, *The Female Advantage: Women's Ways of Leadership* (New York: Doubleday Currency, 1990), 5–68. What Helgesen noted in 1990 has turned out to be increasingly desirable in the twenty-first century. More corporations want CEOs with web-inclusive-interactive styles of leadership rather than top-down authoritarian styles of leadership. Helgesen reflects this in her more recent work, *Everyday Revolutionaries: Working Women and the Transformation of American Life* (New York: Doubleday, 1998). The same reality is reflected in Rosenthal's *When Women Lead,* cited above.

30. K. Bussey and B. Maughan report that men reasoned differently depending on the sex of the person to whom they were speaking. Men tended to score at stage 3 when they talked with a woman but at stage 4 when they talked with a man. Women, on the other hand, did not change their mode of reasoning as a function of the sex of the person to whom they were speaking. See Susan Basow, *Gender Stereotypes and Roles* (Pacific Grove, Calif.: Brooks/Cole Publishing, 1992), 65.

31. Carol Tavris, *The Mismeasure of Woman* (New York: Simon & Schuster, 1993), 89.

32. Thelma J. Goodrich, Cheryl Rampage, Barbara Ellman, and Kris Halstead, *Feminist Family Therapy: A Case Book* (New York: W. W. Norton, 1988), 20.

33. See H. Richard Niebuhr, *The Responsible Self: An Essay in Christian Moral Philosophy* (San Francisco: Harper & Row, 1963).

34. For readers interested in pursuing this question beyond the Gilligan and Niebuhr books, an extended discussion of this relational challenge to Enlightenment moral philosophy is found in Susan J. Hekman, *Moral Voices, Moral Selves* (Cambridge, U.K.: Polity Press, 1995).

35. Elizabeth Achtemeier, "Righteousness," in *The Interpreter's Dictionary of the Bible,* vol. 4 (New York: Abingdon Press, 1962), 80–85.

36. Ruth Tiffany Barnhouse, *A Woman's Identity* (Cleveland, S.C.: Bonne Chance Press, 1994), 47.

Chapter 3

1. The ancient Jewish rabbis counted 613 separate commandments in the law, and they debated which was the greatest. So when they approached Jesus (Matt. 22:36–40), their question was, "Teacher, which is the great commandment in the law?" Jesus' answer matched the best Jewish thought, and in Mark's account (12:29–34), the scribe asking the question marveled at Jesus' answer and said, "Teacher, you have spoken the truth." This Great Commandment is for both Jews and Christians the summary of God's primary requirement. It turns the negatives of the Ten Commandments into a positive (see George Arthur Buttrick, ed., *The Interpreter's Bible: A Commentary in Twelve Volumes,* vol. 2 [New York: Abingdon Press, 1953], 372–73).

2. Ibid., 372. In Deuteronomy 9:23–24, Moses reminds the Israelites, "Likewise, when the LORD sent you from Kadesh Barnea, saying, 'Go up and possess the land which I have given you,' then you rebelled against the commandment of the LORD your God, and you did not believe Him nor obey His voice. You have been rebellious against the LORD from the day that I knew you."

3. *The Interpreter's Dictionary of the Bible,* vol. 4 (New York: Abingdon Press, 1962), 428–29.

4. Ibid., 428.

5. Ibid., 429.

6. *The International Standard Bible Encyclopedia,* vol. 5 (Grand Rapids: Eerdmans, 1952), 2837–38.

7. The Greek word used by Matthew, Mark, and Luke is not the common word *pas* for "all," used in a quantitative sense. It is *holos,* meaning "whole" or "entire." It has a qualitative feel.

8. In no way is this a criticism of counseling services. Such services have given many people a new and better way to think about their attitudes and actions in relationship to others.

9. M. Gay Hubbard, *Women: The Misunderstood Majority* (Waco: Word, 1992), 1, 8.

10. L. I. Pearlin and C. Schooler, "The Structure of Coping," *Journal of Health and Social Behavior* 22 (1978): 337–56.

11. For an extended discussion of this, see Susan Basow, *Gender Stereotypes and Roles,* 3d ed. (Pacific Grove, Calif.: Brooks/Cole Publishing, 1992), 172–202.

12. Pearlin and Schooler, "Structure of Coping," 342. The self-talk involved in managing emotions may for a woman include, for example, denying the anger she feels because she believes that anger is not a legitimate emotion for a Christian. She may insist to others that she is not angry, but this exacerbates the stress as it cuts her off from a part of her own reality.

13. New ongoing studies on the stress differentials between men and women are positing other explanations for women's higher levels of stress. According to Judy Foreman, females tend to pay for the "cost of caring." She cited psychologist Alice Domar at the Mind/Body Medical Institute at Beth Israel Deaconess Medical Center in Boston, who said, "Men worry about three things—their immediate family, their job and money. Women worry on a daily basis about up to 12 things—their immediate family, their job, money, their extended family, their friends, their kids' friends, the way the house looks, their weight, the dog, etc." Ronald Kessler, sociologist and health care policy professor at Harvard Medical School, noted that "women have more bad stuff going on. It's the coordination that kills you, and when something gives, it's the woman who fills the gap." Judy Foreman, "Stressed Out? Try a Hug," *The Boston Globe,* 13 August 2002, p. D3.

14. In chapter 1, the question was raised whether the differences we think we see between men and women are innate (that we're born a certain way) or developed over time as we grow up in particular cultures. This is an important question because, as noted in chapter 1, we do grow up in diverse subcultures. For example, men tend to score slightly higher than women on measures of global self-esteem. But this gender difference turns out to be stronger among Euro-American women than among African American women, with white women showing the lowest self-esteem. Basow reports a national study (American Association of University Women, "Shortchanging Girls, Shortchanging America" [Washington, D.C.: The Greenberg-Lake Analysis Group, 1991]) of more than three thousand fourth- through tenth-grade students in which the gender differences in self-esteem widen when children move from elementary school to middle school. For girls, agreement with the statement "I'm happy the way I am" dropped from 60 percent in grade school to 37 percent in middle school to 29 percent in high school. On the other hand, boys agreed with the statement 67 percent of the time in grade school, 56 percent during middle school, and 46 percent in high school. It is important to note that for the girls, the largest decrease in self-esteem was among white and Hispanic girls, and the smallest decrease was among African American girls. Something other than a person's sex is also at work in the area of self-esteem. Explanations of these apparent differences in self-esteem between men and women will likely lie not in biology but in the social contexts in which men and women live their lives.

15. David Neff, *Christianity Today,* 22 July 1991, 13.

16. Peggy Orenstein, *School Girls: Young Women, Self-Esteem, and the Confidence Gap* (New York: Doubleday, 1994) in association with the American Association of University Women study cited in note 9.

17. Mary Pipher, *Reviving Ophelia: Saving the Selves of Adolescent Girls* (New York: Putnam, 1994).

18. An important resource for anyone interested in further reading in this area is William Pollack, *Real Boys: Rescuing Our Sons from the Myths of Boyhood* (New York: Henry Holt, 1998). Another important resource is the 1998 Horatio Alger Association report, suggesting that males are actually in a downward turn academically and in areas associated with self-esteem and expectations for the future. In some cases, they now score lower than girls. This information was reported in Pollack, *Real Boys,* 173.

19. Basow, *Gender Stereotypes,* 174.

20. Some Christians object to the term *self*-esteem, reminding one another that only *God*-esteem should be our goal. However, God created us as selves in his image, and we are called to live in the tension of being redeemed and gifted selves in the midst of our total dependence on God.

21. In no way do I want to imply that all depressions are alike. Physicians distinguish several types of depression for which treatment is not identical. *Dysthymia* is the least severe form of depression, often long-term with chronic symptoms. It is not fully disabling but prevents sufferers from functioning at peak. *Major depression* interferes with the ability to work, sleep, eat, and enjoy life. This kind of depression occurs in women twice as often as in men, with 11 percent of the U.S. population affected yearly. It occurs more often in people in cities (as opposed to rural settings), and the people at highest risk are young women who have small children and minimal support in child-rearing. *Bipolar depression* is disabling, with a cycling between depression and elation leading to irrational actions. It is not as common as unipolar depression. A fourth form of depression is *seasonal affective disorder,* common in winter with little sunshine. Women may go through *postpartum depression* after the birth of a baby, and most of us experience *grief reaction bereavement* when we lose someone we love. The use of the term *depression* as a general category, therefore, can be misleading.

22. Margaret W. Matlin, *The Psychology of Women,* 3d ed. (Orlando, Fla.: Harcourt Brace, 1996), 453. To support these statistics, Matlin cites the following studies: R. C. Kessler, K. A. McGonagle, S. Zhao, C. B. Nelson, M. Hughes, S. Eshleman, H. Wittchen, and K. S. Kendler, "Lifetime and 12-month Prevalence of DSM-III-R Psychiatric Disorders in the United States," *Archives of General Psychiatry* 51 (1994): 8–19; and E. McGrath, G. P. Keita, B. R. Strickland, and N. F. Russo, eds., *Women and Depression* (Washington, D.C.: American Psychological Association, 1990). The statistic may mask the fact that men are more likely than women to use drugs and alcohol (rather than therapy) to cope with depression, leading to higher rates of substance abuse in men and higher rates of depression in women.

23. Our culture gives women permission to be sick and to seek help for both physical and mental illnesses in ways that men cannot.

24. See Dana Crowley Jack, *Silencing the Self: Women and Depression* (Cambridge: Harvard University Press, 1991), 1. E. D. Rothblum commented that "the lifetime risk for developing depression ranges from 2 percent to 12 percent for men and from 5.5 percent to 26 percent for women" (E. D. Rothblum, "Women's Socializaton and the Prevalence of Depression: The Feminine Mistake," *Women and Therapy* 1 [1982]: 5–13). See also P. J. Wickramaratne, M. M. Weissman, P. J. Leaf, and T. R. Holford, "Age, Period, and Cohort Effects on the Risk of Major Depression: Results from Five United States Communities," *Journal of Clinical Epidemiology* 42 (1989): 333–43.

25. Matlin, *Psychology of Women,* 454.

26. Jack, *Silencing the Self,* 6.

27. Ibid., 7

28. Sigmund Freud commented that "normally, there is nothing of which we are more certain than the feeling of our self, of our own ego. This ego appears to us as something autonomous and

unitary, marked off distinctly from everything else" (Sigmund Freud, *Civilization and Its Discontents,* trans. J. Strachey [1930; reprint, New York: W. W. Norton, 1961], 13).

29. B. Ehrenreich and D. English, *For Her Own Good: 150 Years of the Experts' Advice to Women* (New York: Doubleday/Anchor, 1979), 274–75.

30. Jack, *Silencing the Self,* 9.

31. Roy McCloughry, *Men and Masculinity: From Power to Love* (London: Hodder & Stoughton, 1992), 253.

32. S. A. Mitchell observed that "there is no 'self' in a psychologically meaningful sense, in isolation, outside a matrix of relations with others" (*Relational Concepts in Psychoanalysis: An Integration* [Cambridge: Harvard University Press, 1988], 33). Readers who want to pursue this may also want to read the work of sociologist Herbert Blumer in the area of symbolic interactionism.

33. Nancy Chodorow, *The Reproduction of Mothering: Psychoanalysis and the Sociology of Gender* (Berkeley: University of California Press, 1978), 167.

34. Matlin, *Psychology of Women,* 458–59.

35. For example, in the area of verbal communication, see L. McMullen, "Sex Differences in Spoken Language: Empirical Truth or Mythic Truth?" (paper presented at the annual convention of the Canadian Psychological Association, Quebec City, Canada, 1992), for evidence that men interrupt women far more than women interrupt men; M. LaFrance, "Gender and Interruptions: Individual Infraction or Violation of the Social Order?" *Psychology of Women Quarterly* 16 (1992): 497–512, reported that women are evaluated negatively when they interrupt a man, but men are not so evaluated; K. Bischoping, "Gender Differences in Conversation Topics, 1922–1990," *Sex Roles* 28 (1993): 1–18, found that men are significantly more likely than women to talk about sports and entertainment, and women talk about men four times more than men talk about women. In the area of facial expression, J. M. Stoppard and C. D. G. Gruchy, "Gender, Context, and Expression of Positive Emotion," *Personality and Social Psychology Bulletin* 19 (1993): 143–50, reported that women are expected to smile and express positive emotion toward other people, but there is no such rule for men. These and many other reported differences are discussed in Matlin, *Psychology of Women,* 213–29.

36. This section reports various gender differences in communication patterns that have held up in a variety of studies. Matlin (*Psychology of Women,* 215) observes, however, that the size of gender difference depends on at least four possible factors:

1. Gender differences are largest when behavior is assessed in terms of self-report. People often describe themselves as "more nurturant," "more cognitive," etc., than objective measurements would corroborate.

2. Gender differences are largest when other people are present (e.g., men might act especially heroic when a crowd of onlookers has gathered).

3. Gender differences are largest when the behavior requires specific gender-related skills (such as changing a tire or cooking a meal).

4. Gender differences are largest when gender is prominent and other roles are minimized: At a conference of accountants, where professional roles are emphasized, men and women are likely to act similarly.

For an extended evaluation of the scientific literature on gender differences, see Elizabeth Aries, *Men and Women in Interaction: Reconsidering the Differences* (New York: Oxford University Press, 1996).

37. Matlin, *Psychology of Women,* 216.

38. Ibid.

39. Virginia Sapiro, *Women in American Society* (Palo Alto, Calif.: Mayfield Publishing, 1986), 278.

40. J. Coates, "Epistemic Modality and Spoken Discourse," *Transactions of the Philological Society* (1987): 110–31, cited in Aries, *Men and Women,* 117.

41. For a variety of citations with discussion, see any of the following texts: Janet Shibley Hyde, *Half the Human Experience: The Psychology of Women,* 4th ed. (Lexington, Mass.: D. C. Heath, 1991), 87–106; Sapiro, *Women in American Society,* 270–90; Basow, *Gender Stereotypes,* 57–62; and Matlin, *Psychology of Women,* 212–55.

42. Women tend to add various types of disclaimers to their speech, extending sentences; men, on the other hand, tend to speak in declarative sentences without disclaimers such as "I may be wrong, but . . ." or after a sentence adding, "I don't know if this makes sense to you."

43. Aries, *Men and Women,* 135–44.

44. For a scholarly discussion of the shortcomings of some of the popular literature on gender difference, see ibid., 3–23. Aries notes that John Gray's book *Men Are from Mars, Women Are from Venus* (New York: HarperCollins, 1992) relies heavily on participants' reports in relationship seminars, and Deborah Tannen's book, *You Just Don't Understand: Men and Women in Conversation* (London: Virago, 1991), relies on anecdotal accounts. Neither work systematically addresses the large body of interdisciplinary research on gender and communication that has come out in the last quarter century.

45. I am indebted to Virginia Sapiro for this analogy.

46. Natalie Porter and Florence Geis, "Women and Nonverbal Leadership Cues: When Seeing Is Not Believing," in *Gender and Nonverbal Behavior,* ed. Clara Mayo and Nancy Henley (New York: Springer-Verlag, 1981), 39–62.

47. For example, Pollack, *Real Boys* explores the myths of masculinization of boys and their effect on male self-understanding.

48. Mary Stewart Van Leeuwen, *Gender and Grace: Love, Work, and Parenting in a Changing World* (Downers Grove, Ill.: InterVarsity Press, 1990), 89–105.

49. Hubbard, *Women,* 4.

50. W. R. Gove, "Mental Illness and Psychiatric Treatment among Women," in *Psychology of Women: Ongoing Debates,* ed. Mary Roth Walsh (New Haven: Yale University Press, 1987), 110.

51. Basow, *Gender Stereotypes,* 186. See also E. Walker, B. A. Bettes, E. K. Kain, and P. Harvey, "Relationship of Gender and Marital Status with Symptomatology in Psychotic Patients," *Journal of Abnormal Psychology* 94 (1985): 42–50.

52. While women seek counseling and clinical help more than men do, the DSM-III-R reports that men are prone to more varied mental disorders than women, with males having more difficulties in childhood, and females "catching up" in adolescence (ages 14 or 15) and eventually passing male rates of psychological disorder.

53. R. Helson and J. Picano, "Is the Traditional Role Bad for Women?" *Journal of Personality and Social Psychology* 59 (1990): 311–20; cited in Basow, *Gender Stereotypes,* 199.

54. Francis Purifoy and Lambert Koopmans, "Androstenedione, Testosterone, and Free Testosterone Concentration in Women of Various Occupations," *Social Biology* 26 (1980): 179–80.

55. Basow, *Gender Stereotypes,* 185. In support, Basow cites W. Gove, "Sex Differences in the Epidemiology of Mental Disorder: Evidence and Explanations," in *Gender and Disordered Behavior: Sex Differences in Psychopathology,* ed. E. S. Gomberg and V. Franks (New York: Brunner/Mazel, 1979), 23–68; W. R. Gove, "Mental Illness and Psychiatric Treatment among Women," *Psychology of Women Quarterly* 4 (1980): 345–62; and N. F. Russo, "Overview: Forging Research Priorities for Women's Mental Health," *American Psychologist* 45 (1990): 368–73.

56. G. L. Klerman and M. M. Weissman, "Increasing Rates of Depression," *Journal of the American Medical Association* 261 (1989): 2229–35; see also G. L. Klerman, M. M. Weissman, B. J. Rounsaville, and E. S. Chevron, *Interpersonal Psychotherapy of Depression* (New York: Basic Books, 1984); and Weissman and Klerman, "Sex Differences," 98–111.

57. See Haddon Robinson, *Biblical Preaching,* 2d ed. (Grand Rapids: Baker, 2001), 94–96.

58. Robert R. Howard, "Gender and Point of View in the Imagery of Preaching," *Homiletic* 24, no. 1 (summer 1999): 1.

59. *Pulpit Digest* (January/February 1991), cited in ibid., 5.

60. Howard, "Gender and Point of View," 5.

61. Preachers who would like to include more female examples in their preaching but need some resources will find numerous books in Christian bookstores on women in the Bible. Some may want to consult my book *A Woman God Can Lead: Lessons from Women of the Bible Help You Make Today's Choices* (Grand Rapids: Discovery House, 1998). (This volume combines two earlier books published by Discovery House: *A Woman God Can Use,* 1990, and *A Woman Jesus Can Teach,* 1991.)

Chapter 4

1. These questions and definitions are taken from Mary Field Belenky, Blythe McVicker Clinchy, Nancy Rule Goldberger, and Jill Mattuck Tarule, *Women's Ways of Knowing: The Development of Self, Voice, and Mind* (New York: Basic Books, 1986), 3. The social science analysis in chapters 4, 5, and 6 owes much to the work of Belenky and her colleagues.

2. The second (Is it true?) of the three functional questions dealing with persuasion is wrapped up in epistemology. For an extended discussion of the three functional questions and their importance for preaching, see Haddon Robinson, *Biblical Preaching*, 2d ed. (Grand Rapids: Baker, 2001), 115–24.

3. See D. Bakan, *The Duality of Human Existence* (Boston: Beacon Press, 1966); also see Nancy Chodorow, *The Reproduction of Mothering* (Berkeley: University of California Press, 1978); and C. McMillan, *Women, Reason, and Nature* (Princeton, N.J.: Princeton University Press, 1982).

4. Carroll Smith-Rosenberg, *Disorderly Conduct: Visions of Gender in Victorian America* (New York: Oxford University Press, 1985), 23; see also 182–96.

5. William Perry, *Forms of Intellectual and Ethical Development in the College Years* (New York: Holt, Rinehart, and Winston, 1968).

6. Stage 1: Men begin as *basic dualists,* viewing the world in polarities of right/wrong, we/they, good/bad. They are passive learners, dependent on outside authorities to hand down truth to them, teaching them what to believe.

Stage 2: Gradually, men become aware of the diversity of opinions and multiple perspectives other people hold. This shakes their dualistic faith in absolute authority and truth. Dualism gives way to *multiplicity*. In this stage, men begin to understand that human authorities may not always have the right answer. They grow beyond a dependency on and trust in only external authorities and carve out their own territory of personal mental freedom.

Stage 3: In pursuing higher education, a male student often finds his opinions challenged by a professor's insistence on evidence and support for his opinion. At this point, multiplicity yields to a third way of knowing that Perry called *relativity subordinate*. In this stage, the student actively and consciously cultivates an analytical, evaluative approach to knowledge. He learns to weigh arguments and marshal points to support what he believes to be true.

Stage 4: Finally, at some point, men may come to believe that truth is relative. At this point, they shift into *full relativism*. They accept that the meaning of an event depends on the context in which the event occurs and on the framework used to understand the event. They also come to believe that knowledge is constructed, not given. Human knowledge is contextual, not absolute. It is mutable, not fixed. For Perry, only at the point of full relativism can we affirm and commit to our personal identity.

7. Belenky et al., *Women's Ways of Knowing.* While some social scientists have taken issue with various aspects of the Belenky research project, the broad understanding of women's epistemologies (and how they may differ at certain points from those of men) has helped me sort out numerous issues in ministry to women.

8. By limiting his study to students at Harvard University, Perry may have overlooked a similar group of men in the wider culture. We cannot say that men who are mindless and voiceless do not exist; we can say only that Perry did not have such a category among those whom he studied.

9. Parts of this discussion were taken from Belenky et al., *Women's Ways of Knowing,* 15–34. Readers interested in exploring in greater detail the epistemology of silence are encouraged to consult this book.

10. Perry called these men *basic dualists,* emphasizing their either-or way of thinking, whereas Belenky and her colleagues called these women *received knowers,* emphasizing that the sources of their knowledge are always outside themselves. For a full discussion of this epistemological perspective, see ibid., 35–51.

11. Belenky et al., *Women's Ways of Knowing,* 35–51.

12. This attitude is cultivated in many church circles. While churches may teach the doctrine of the perspicuity of Scripture, they also buttress the idea that laypeople need study Bibles with study notes, and they need authoritative teachers.

13. This crisis of trust can be precipitated by any number of events or circumstances: If a woman perceives that an authority figure has lied to her or has misrepresented truth, that may be enough to trigger an epistemological change. Moral failure on the part of the authority figure can also do this, as can any violent or violating act (such as rape, sexual harassment, etc.).

14. To explore subjective knowing, see Belenky et al., *Women's Ways of Knowing,* 52–86, from which information in this section was taken.

15. Ibid., 77.

16. M. Gay Hubbard, *Women: The Misunderstood Majority* (Dallas: Word, 1992), 105.

17. See Robinson, *Biblical Preaching,* 115–24.

18. It is lamentable that in many Christian circles today, "Bible study" focuses exclusively on the third functional question of application. That can be quicksand for the unsuspecting Christian who has not first learned to ask what the text itself means before moving to an application that may or may not be justified by the text. Examples of this abound whenever a verse is taken out of context and used as a promise from God in ways the text does not warrant (e.g., using Matt. 18:19–20 as a promise related to group prayer when the context is clearly about church discipline, dealing with a brother who has sinned against you).

19. It was this approach in C. S. Lewis's *Mere Christianity* that helped me see the importance of the second functional question in persuasion. Many listeners need to know that the speaker has also wrestled seriously with their questions and has found solid answers.

20. Samuel P. Huntington, *American Politics: The Promise of Disharmony* (Cambridge: Harvard University Press, 1981), 65.

21. Ibid., 64.

22. The issue of the abuse of women has been trivialized in many churches. It is possible that the revelations of the sexual abuse of boys by priests in certain Roman Catholic dioceses will help Christians everywhere recognize that other Christian leaders may also be guilty of abusing women and children who are physically weaker or have lesser status.

23. Max Weber, *The Sociology of Religion,* trans. Ephraim Fischoff (1922; reprint, Boston: Beacon Press, 1963).

Chapter 5

1. Charles Dickens, *A Tale of Two Cities* (1859). The full quotation opening the book is also appropriate to this chapter: "It was the best of times, it was the worst of times, it was the age of wisdom, it was the age of foolishness, it was the epoch of belief, it was the epoch of incredulity, it was the season of Light, it was the season of Darkness, it was the spring of hope, it was the winter of despair, we had everything before us, we had nothing before us, we were all going direct to Heaven, we were all going direct the other way—in short, the period was so far like the present period, that some of its noisiest authorities insisted on its being received, for good or for evil, in the superlative degree of comparison only."

2. I do not personally feel that postmodernism is responsible for much that we decry in our culture today, as will become evident in the discussion in this chapter.

3. Both the Apostles' Creed and the Nicene Creed include the description of the church as "universal," as it appeared to be from the time of Constantine until the Reformation.

4. Peter Berger, *The Sacred Canopy* (New York: Anchor Books/Doubleday, 1967), 111–12.

5. The earliest thinkers who contributed to the Enlightenment lived in the early seventeenth century (Francis Bacon, 1561–1626; René Descartes, 1596–1650; and John Locke, 1632–1704), but Immanuel Kant (1724–1804) and those who followed him brought its ideas to conclusion.

6. I am indebted to Colin Gunton for ideas incorporated into this section of this chapter. See his *Enlightenment and Alienation: An Essay towards a Trinitarian Theology* (Grand Rapids: Eerdmans, 1985).

7. Lesslie Newbigin in the foreword of Gunton's *Enlightenment and Alienation,* vi.

8. Gunton, *Enlightenment and Alienation,* 3–4.

9. Michael Polanyi, *Personal Knowledge: A Post-Critical Philosophy* (London: Routledge and Kegan Paul, 1962), 139.

10. Gunton, *Enlightenment and Alienation,* 2, referring to Hans-Georg Gadamer, *Truth and Method* (New York: Seabury Press, 1975), 266.

11. This section draws mainly on the work of George Marsden, in particular chapter 1, "Evangelical America at the Brink of Crisis," in his *Fundamentalism and American Culture: The Shaping of Twentieth Century Evangelicalism 1870–1925* (New York: Oxford University Press, 1980). See this chapter for a full discussion of Scottish Common Sense Realism and the way it played out among nineteenth-century evangelical Protestants' beliefs about the verification of Scripture by science.

12. Ibid., 16.

13. Ibid.

14. Peter Berger, "Toward a Critique of Modernity," in *Religion and the Sociology of Knowledge: Modernization and Pluralism in Christian Thought and Structure,* ed. Barbara Hargrove (New York: Edward Mellon Press, 1984). In this essay, Berger discusses modernity as characterized by five dilemmas:

The first dilemma we face is *a sense of alienation.* Mobility tore people from the relatively cohesive communities in which people found support, solidarity, and meaning throughout most of history. The Industrial Revolution lured fathers and other family members out of the villages and off the farms with the promise of regular wages in place of subsistence living. The process eroded the familial economic unit as nothing else has. The factory production system split work into small repetitive tasks, which denied workers a sense of accomplishment for the end product. What mattered was mass production: How can we get the most units per hour with the most efficiency? A loss of the deep human relationships we yearn for is one price we pay for living in modern times.

A second dilemma brought to us by modernity is *a change in the way we think about time.* For centuries, people focused on the past and the present; we focus on the future. This has changed the rhythm of our lives. To the premodern Chinese, a clock was a toy. Baudelaire called the clock "*un Dieu sinistre, effrayant, impossible*"—a sinister, terrifying, impossible god. But we strap a miniature time machine to our wrist every day and allow that machine to govern our lives. This is in sharp contrast to the way human beings experienced time before the advent of the modern period. Modernity brought a powerful shift in attention from the past to the future. So we live life as a "career" as we map our projects in terms of a plan (one-year, five-year, ten-year). Psychologists tell us that this pace of modern living damages our mental and physical well-being. Yet we see no way out of the endless striving, the restlessness, and our mounting incapacity for repose. Time is not our ally. It has become our enemy, keeping us from building the relationships we want and need. It keeps us striving to get ahead instead of being grateful for our present situation.

A third dilemma posed by modernity is *the progressive separation of individuals from the group.* In premodern societies, the all-embracing, all-containing communities did not let go. But now, for the most part, such communities are gone. We can come and go as we please and few people care.

At the same time that our concrete communities have been replaced by the abstract megastructures of modern society, we have come to experience ourselves as both separate and simultaneously in greater need of personal belonging. We are ambiguous about our twin desires—we want our personal autonomy at the same time that we want community. It makes us ask whether the modern idea of the individual as an *individual* is a great step forward in the story of human growth or a dehumanizing aberration.

The fourth dilemma brought to us by modernity is *the vastly increased range of options open to us in today's world.* It is the gift and the problem of choice. Years ago people saw life as being dominated by fate; today they see almost unlimited choice. One of the most seductive maxims of the times is that things can be other than what they have been. As moderns, we embrace that. We have been drawn into the turbulent dynamism of modernity with its insatiable thirst for innovation. In this mind-set, what is today is always better than what was yesterday or last year. Tradition is no longer binding because we can change whatever we want to change. The future is an open horizon. One of the most ancient functions of society was to take away from individuals the burden of choice, but with modernization, this "unburdening" function of society was weakened. In the process, both individual and collective life came to be more and more uncertain. This "liberation" is both exhilarating and terrifying. We wonder what are the limits, if any, to this "freedom." How do we provide stability in an age of such dynamic uncertainties? This liberation from all boundaries limiting choice is one of the most powerful inspirations of modernity. Its price tag is the "anguish of choice" described well by the existentialists. We end up with that strangely modern paradox called "escape from freedom" about which Erich Fromm wrote—an escape from having to choose. So we find ourselves with two ideals of freedom: liberation *as* choice and liberation *from* choice; freedom *to* choose and freedom *from having to* choose. Both ideals crisscross our modern values and ideologies.

The fifth dilemma we live with is *secularization.* Modern scientific inquiry introduced a massive threat to the plausibility of religious belief and experience. In the latter part of the nineteenth century, the split between religion and science was complete when "knowledge" was no longer allowed to include what could not be verified scientifically. All that is transcendent in human experience was excluded from "objective knowledge." Yet all people (Christian and otherwise) want to exist in a meaningful and ultimately hopeful cosmos. We need satisfactory ways of explaining and coping with suffering and evil in human life.

15. It is important to state that while the various epistemologies may appear to be stages, with transitions from one to the next, this is not a trajectory model. Both the Perry and Belenky studies appear to be somewhat additive, with new kinds of knowing being added to what was already there. The exception would be the shift from received to subjective knower. But most of us continue to know some things by receiving them from those we consider to be experts while also knowing other things by analysis or by synthesis. We may also continue to be dualistic in some areas of thinking while accommodating more complex forms of knowing in other areas of thinking.

16. Mary Field Belenky, Blythe McVicker Clinchy, Nancy Rule Goldberger, and Jill Mattuck Tarule, *Women's Ways of Knowing: The Development of Self, Voice, and Mind* (New York: Basic Books, 1986), 26.

17. It is at this point that some difference between men and women begins to surface. In Perry's account of intellectual development, his male students discovered critical reasoning as a means to win the academic game. For them, this new way of thinking or knowing was to be used to construct powerful arguments for or against an idea. Basic to procedural knowing is the ability to marshal arguments in such a way that the individual can win a debate. At its heart is critical thinking or, as Peter Elbow calls it, "the doubting game" (Peter Elbow, *Writing without Teachers* [London: Oxford University Press, 1973], 173). Procedural knowers, when presented with a proposition, immediately look for something *wrong* with it—a loophole, a factual error, a logical contradiction, or the omission of contrary evidence. Belenky found, on the other hand, that women who are procedural or analytical knowers often do not see doubting as a "game." Such women tend to think

of arguments as being between *people*, not between *ideas,* and they fear that someone will get hurt. We must stop short, however, of inferring that all men play the doubting game and all women do not. Procedural knowers are tough-minded, in Belenky's words. They assume that everyone can be wrong. As they develop techniques for analyzing and evaluating arguments, they become less vulnerable to attack. Ibid., 104.

18. Ibid., 113.

19. Ibid., 127.

20. As Perry worked with the boys and men in his research, he saw some move to what he called *full relativism,* meaning that the person comes to believe that truth is relative, that the meaning of an event depends on the context in which that event occurs and on the framework the knower uses to understand that event. This relativism pervades all aspects of life, not just the academic world. For the person in this category, knowledge is constructed, not given; it is contextual, not absolute; it is mutable, not fixed.

21. In this they differed markedly from Perry's men, for whom the single clarifying and self-defining act was the choice of a career. Much less frequently did Perry find men talking about moral values and relationships. This is corroborated by George Vaillant's longitudinal study of the male adult life cycle in which he noted that for men up to middle age, idealism and intimacy take a backseat to the quest for career: "Having achieved intimacy with a few fellow humans, he then tries to run faster and in a slightly different direction from all his classmates" (George Vaillant, *Adaptation to Life* [Boston: Little Brown, 1977], 217; cited in ibid., 150).

22. It seems accurate that certain kinds of churches and certain types of preaching appeal to certain kinds of listeners. What draws one group of knowers may repel another group. Some churches put a great deal of emphasis on charismatic experience or worship. In other churches, the sermon or the Eucharist is central. Parishioners often judge churches on the basis of music or worship or preaching. For pastors interested in studying these differences further, I strongly recommend Richard Foster's *Streams of Living Water: Celebrating the Great Traditions of Christian Faith* (San Francisco: HarperSan Francisco, 1998). In this meaty 448-page book, Foster examines theologically, historically, and sociologically each of the major Christian emphases (worship, Word, Spirit, holiness, social concern, etc.) as they have impacted the development of various denominations and individual churches.

Chapter 6

1. Quoted by Elisabeth Elliot in *A Chance to Die: The Life and Legacy of Amy Carmichael* (Old Tappan, N.J.: Revell, 1987), 221.

2. While no task is insignificant when done to honor God, I have seen seminary-trained women with a mission organization confined to "gofer" jobs in the ministry. Years of work no more challenging than running errands and typing church bulletins eventually caused these women to leave the mission for ministry more in line with their gifts and training. Recently, a woman who is a seminary graduate and serves on a church staff full-time in a ministry position told me, "In contrast to other members of the church staff, I'm paid like a secretary and I'm treated like a secretary."

3. The cultural seduction of Christian women is evident in many venues. I have spoken at church-sponsored women's events in which informal conversation (as well as much of the planned programs) focused on wardrobes, the tennis club, and next week's party, to the exclusion of any sense of spiritual need. Those who plan such events are themselves caught up in fashion and fun with no evident awareness of eternal values.

4. Christ quotes from Elie Wiesel, *The Town beyond the Wall*, trans. Steven Becker (New York: Avon Books, 1970), 190.

5. Carol Christ, *Laughter of Aphrodite: Reflections on a Journey to the Goddess* (San Francisco: Harper & Row, 1987), 30.

6. Ibid., 191.

7. Benedict J. Groeschel, in *Spiritual Passages: The Psychology of Spiritual Development* (New York: Crossroad, 1996), describes the spiritual life as "the sum total of responses which one makes to what is perceived as the inner call of God" (4).

8. Joann Wolski Conn, *Women's Spirituality: Resources for Christian Development* (New York: Paulist Press, 1986), 3.

9. Mary Field Belenky, Blythe McVicker Clinchy, Nancy Rule Goldberger, and Jill Mattuck Tarule, *Women's Ways of Knowing: The Development of Self, Voice, and Mind* (New York: Basic Books, 1986), 23.

10. Ibid., 29.

11. Ibid., 32.

12. Lev Vygotsky, *Mind in Society: The Development of Higher Psychological Processes* (Cambridge: Harvard University Press, 1978), cited in Belenky et al., *Women's Ways of Knowing*, 32–33.

13. Belenky et al., *Women's Ways of Knowing*, 41.

14. Ibid., 42.

15. As a seminary professor, I have noted that in deciding which courses to take, students with this epistemology want to know exactly how many tests will be given, how many papers they will have to write, and how long the papers will have to be. They want to know how many pages of how many books they will have to read and how their grades will be computed. And they think that grades should take the form of hourly wages: the longer they work, the higher the grade.

16. Received knowers listen only to outside voices for truth, never processing truth internally to make it their own. This has two negative consequences. The first is that they tend to judge others by the truth they have received externally without allowing for divergent interpretations or opinions. The second consequence is that their spirituality is shallow, dependent on external props, because they do not have the capacity to internalize it.

17. Carol Gilligan, *In a Different Voice* (Cambridge: Harvard University Press, 1982), cited in Belenky et al., *Women's Ways of Knowing*, 46; see also M. S. Horner, "Toward an Understanding of Achievement-Related Conflicts in Women," *Journal of Social Issues* 28 (1972): 157–76; J. B. Miller, *Towards a New Psychology of Women* (Boston: Beacon Press, 1976); and G. Sassen, "Success Anxiety in Women: A Constructivist Interpretation of Its Source and Its Significance," *Harvard Education Review* 50 (1980): 13–24.

18. Belenky et al., *Women's Ways of Knowing*, 58.

19. Quoted in ibid., 61.

20. Ibid., 82. Belenky noted that this birth of the self in subjective knowers can occur at virtually any age, as late as 30 or 40, even at 50.

21. This belief (explored in chap. 4) was widely proclaimed throughout most of the nineteenth century in popular women's magazines and in sermons as part of the doctrine of separate spheres. Physicians endorsed it, stating that thinking destroyed a woman's capacity to feel, just as emotional display destroyed a man's capacity to think.

22. Belenky et al., *Women's Ways of Knowing*, 69.

23. Ibid., 70

24. Ibid., 85.

25. As pointed out in chapter 5, however, in the lives of men and women, procedural knowledge may take different forms. It can be "separate" or it can be "connected" procedural knowledge. In both, the knowers think systematically, using the tools of logic and analysis. But the separate procedural knower plays the "doubting game" (looking for loopholes or flaws in someone else's argument), whereas the connected procedural knower plays the "believing game," trying to understand the author's viewpoint and conclusions. Some women are separate procedural knowers, though more often this is the perspective adopted by men. In contrast to separate procedural knowers, connected procedural knowers use empathy (not argument) in order to understand another person's ideas and to try to get inside the experience that led the other person to form the idea.

Although these women (and the men who are connected procedural knowers) play the doubting game as part of the process of analysis, believing feels more real to them than doubting. For these knowers, deep relationships are the ground from which this knowledge springs.

26. A word of caution: There appears to be a certain progression in the epistemologies examined in chapters 4, 5, and 6, but this must not be confused with spiritual or intellectual maturity. While a procedural knower or a constructed knower may have a richer intellectual life, this does not necessarily imply a higher level of maturity. Probably all of us know received knowers who show great maturity—and constructed knowers who do not. The latter epistemologies seem to provide the seedbed for a richer understanding of God, but certainly not all procedural or constructed knowers allow the seed of the Word of God to take root in their lives and produce a spiritual maturity.

27. Simone Weil, *Waiting for God* (New York: Harper Colophon Books, 1951), 105–16.

28. Belenky et al., *Women's Ways of Knowing,* 150.

29. Conn, *Women's Spirituality,* 3.

30. We all admire women such as Mother Teresa, Florence Nightengale, and others who gave of themselves tirelessly for those who could not help themselves.

31. This is just as true when the genders are reversed. It is no more appropriate for a female speaker to take a cheap shot at men than for a male speaker to go for a laugh at women's expense.

32. J. B. Phillips, *Your God Is Too Small* (New York: Macmillan, 1953). Phillips not only gives his readers a sense of the inadequate visions of God that mislead people but also sets out the vision of a God-sized God in whom people can trust.

33. W. Edward Everding Jr. and Dana W. Wilbanks, *Decision-Making and the Bible* (Valley Forge, Pa.: Judson Press, 1975), 53.

34. Stuart Olyott, quoted in T. M. Moore, *Ecclesiastes: Ancient Wisdom When All Else Fails* (Downers Grove, Ill.: InterVarsity Press, 2001), 112.

35. Frequently, women's stories in the Bible are intertwined with men's stories, and a preacher must decide whose story will be central in a particular sermon. For example, Rahab's story is intertwined with Joshua's story in Joshua 2 and 6. Often the tendency is to go with the man's story, missing an opportunity to connect with women listeners in the pew for whom Rahab's story of faith in action can be a strong encouragement.

36. Aida Besançon Spencer, Donna F. G. Hailson, Catherine Clark Kroeger, and William David Spencer, *The Goddess Revival* (Grand Rapids: Baker, 1995), 19.

Chapter 7

1. Cited in Cheryl Forbes, *The Religion of Power* (Grand Rapids: Zondervan, 1983), 25.

2. Cited in ibid., 51.

3. I take note of the fact that Deuteronomy 6:5 includes loving God with heart, soul, and strength (omitting mind), whereas Jesus in Matthew 22:37 includes loving God with heart, soul, and mind (omitting strength). The lawyer in Luke 10:27 included all four: We are to love God with all our heart, soul, mind, and strength.

4. Joseph Henry Thayer, *A Greek-English Lexicon of the New Testament, Being Grimms' Wilke's Clavis Novi Testamenti* (New York: American Book Co., 1886, 1889), 309. *Ischys* as used in Luke 10:27 means "to the extent of one's ability or strength."

5. A dramatic illustration of this in the American political scene occurred in May 2001 when Vermont's Senator Jeffords left the Republican Party to become an independent, an act that gave Democrats a majority in the Senate. Many power plays had taken place for several years, leading to Jeffords's decision to abandon his party. If you listened to any of the endless commentaries on that action, you more than likely encountered many instances of the abuse of power and its result on the political scene.

6. This is discussed at length (with broad supporting evidence) in Cindy Simon Rosenthal, *When Women Lead: Integrative Leadership in State Legislatures* (New York: Oxford University Press, 1998), chap. 2.

7. See ibid.

8. Ibid., 56–57.

9. Cited in Forbes, *Religion of Power,* 39.

10. It was a short step historically from the Puritan doctrine to the Industrial Revolution and the factory system that enslaved entire families (including small children), making them work on assembly lines for twelve to fourteen hours a day, six days a week. The abuse of power in the name of amassing wealth eventually called for the legislation of Child Labor Laws and other labor controls as well as the rise of labor unions.

11. The term *headship* comes from references in the writings of the apostle Paul to the Corinthian and Ephesian Christians in which he speaks of the husband as the "head" of the wife (1 Cor. 11:3; Eph. 5:23). As scholars have debated the first-century meaning of *kephalē* ("head") in these passages, they have not reached a true consensus as to its meaning. Some argue that the word meant "authority over" in the first century, whereas others cite scholarly reasons to believe that it did not mean "authority over" until the end of the second century. The latter argue that its meaning is "source," not "authority over."

12. Saiving's definition of sin, while not couched in biblical terminology, nevertheless embraces the biblical understanding of pride at the base of sin. Valerie Saiving, "The Human Situation: A Feminine View," in *Womanspirit Rising,* ed. Carol P. Christ and Judith Plaskow (San Francisco: Harper & Row, 1979), 26.

13. Ibid.

14. Susan A. Basow, *Gender Stereotypes and Roles,* 3d ed. (Pacific Grove, Calif.: Brooks/Cole Publishing, 1992), 177.

15. The psalmist uses both *Yahweh* (v. 1) and *Elohim* or *El* with other suffixes (vv. 2, 3) to encompass both God's relationship with his creatures and God's greatness (the plural of majesty and the fullness of divine strength). This is a worthy vision of God to set before his people!

Chapter 8

1. Christians in different churches have differing ideas about women in leadership, and this chapter does not address issues of women in those roles. Rather, it focuses on the type of leadership women tend to give when asked to lead.

2. Cited in Cindy Simon Rosenthal, *When Women Lead: Integrative Leadership in State Legislatures* (New York: Oxford University Press, 1998), chap. 2.

3. I am indebted in this section to Ronald A. Heifetz, *Leadership without Easy Answers* (Cambridge, Mass.: Belknap Press of Harvard University, 1994) for these helpful distinguishing features of various kinds of leadership.

4. John Naisbitt and Patricia Aburdene, *Megatrends 2000: Ten New Directions for the 1990s* (New York: Morrow and Co., 1990), 226.

5. Rosenthal, *When Women Lead,* chap. 2.

6. This analogy was presented by Mary Chapman, corporate trainer at Moody Bible Institute, during a seminar at the National Religious Broadcasters' Midwest Convention, 1998.

7. Rosenthal, *When Women Lead,* chap. 2.

8. Ibid.

9. Cited in Jean Lipman-Blumen, Todd Fryling, Michael C. Henderson, Christine Webster Moore, and Rachel Vecchiotti, *Women in Corporate Leadership: Reviewing a Decade's Research* (Claremont, Calif.: Claremont Graduate University Institute for Advanced Studies in Leadership, the Peter F. Drucker Graduate School of Management, 1996), 31.

10. Ibid., 32.

11. Ibid.

12. Cited in Rosenthal, *When Women Lead,* chap. 2.

13. Edward C. Lehman Jr., *Gender and Work: The Case of the Clergy* (Albany, N.Y.: State University of New York Press, 1993).

14. The four denominations were the American Baptist Convention, the Presbyterian Church USA, the United Church of Christ, and the United Methodist Church. All four denominations have ordained women for many years, yet the study turned up fairly frequent instances of clergywomen experiencing discrimination at the hands of one or more men (whether denominational officials or members of a lay board of the local church). At the same time, under certain conditions, women were as prone as men to use power to get what they wanted.

15. Note the consistency in the application of these differences as described in chapter 2. The basic orientations toward relationships or toward rules in decision-making carry over into church life, politics, and the business world.

16. Sally Helgesen, *The Female Advantage: Women's Ways of Leadership* (New York: Doubleday Currency, 1990), 233–50.

17. The concept of leadership reflected in the remainder of this chapter is drawn directly from Heifetz's understanding of leadership as set forth in *Leadership without Easy Answers.*

18. Chapter 4 explored responses to the gap between an ideal and one's reality. Here the discussion focuses on leading people to see the gap, then leading them to a solution for closing the gap.

19. Heifetz develops this thesis using cases from recent American history to show that there are benefits and liabilities if one leads from a position of power and if one leads from the middle.

20. By "problem" is meant any discontinuity between what is desired and what is experienced. I may desire a closer walk with God than the one I experience. The gap between the two is what is meant here by "problem."

21. Lifestyle problems in a church can include unmarried couples living together, business people in the church cheating on their income tax or taking advantage of employees, physical and sexual abuse within families, people living above their means to impress others, busybodies raising unwarranted questions about others in the congregation, etc.

Chapter 9

1. A hundred years ago, pastors often preached that a woman was not a woman until she married and had a child.

2. Albert Y. Hsu, *Singles at the Crossroads: A Fresh Perspective on Christian Singles* (Downers Grove, Ill.: InterVarsity Press, 1997), 14. He drew his numbers from the U.S. Bureau of the Census, "Current Population Survey: March 1996" (Washington, D.C.: U.S. Government Printing Office, September 1996).

3. The Rutgers University National Marriage Project, "The State of Our Unions: The Social Health of Marriage in America 2001," 1–27.

4. I am indebted to Susan Sletten for some of these insights drawn from her unpublished paper, "Ministering to Single Women," Gordon-Conwell Theological Seminary, December 2001.

5. Hsu, *Singles at the Crossroads,* 24.

6. Ibid., citing David Johnson, "The Pain of Porneia: Singleness and Sexuality, Part 1," sermon preached at Church of the Open Door, Minneapolis, Minnesota, 21 February 1993.

7. Mary Stewart Van Leeuwen, *Gender and Grace: Love, Work, and Parenting in a Changing World* (Downers Grove, Ill.: InterVarsity Press, 1990), 176.

8. Douglas Fagerstrom, ed., *Single Adult Ministry: The Next Step—Seasoned Advice from the Network of Single Adult Leaders* (Wheaton: Victor, 1993), 66.

9. Sletten suggests starting with small mixers and a prayer chain with the hope that married women and single women will find a source of community and strength in one another. Out of this

may grow mentoring relationships and accountability structures ("Ministering to Single Women," 11–13).

10. Betsy Haarmann calls this the "Hope-Despair Continuum"; cited in Beth Spring, *Helping Others in Crisis: The Infertile Couple* (Elgin, Ill.: David C. Cook, 1987), 60.

11. This paragraph draws from an unpublished paper by Annie C. Lee, Gordon-Conwell Theological Seminary, December 2001.

12. Beth Spring, *The Infertile Couple* (Weston, Ont.: David C. Cook, 1987), 17.

13. *Patient's Fact Sheet: Infertility,* American Society for Reproductive Medicine, 14 November 2001.

14. For further discussions of these statistics, see Spring, *Infertile Couple;* Bruce D. Shephard, M.D. and Carroll A. Shephard, R.N., Ph.D., *The Complete Guide to Women's Health* (New York: Plume Books, 1985), 71; and Yvonne S. Thornton, M.D., *Woman to Woman* (New York: Dutton Books, 1997), 117.

15. Information about various treatments for infertility is available at the web site of the American Society for Reproductive Medicine: www.asrm.org/Patients/faqs.html. Follow the links to frequently asked questions about infertility, November 2001.

16. Sandra Glahn and William Cutrer, M.D., *When Empty Arms Become a Heavy Burden: Encouragement for Couples Facing Infertility* (Nashville: Broadman & Holman, 1997), 72.

17. Lee, unpublished paper, 10.

18. Glahn and Cutrer, *Empty Arms,* 17.

19. Historian Betty DeBerg, citing evangelical periodicals of a hundred years ago, provides a sense of the pressure on women to have children during that period. From the *King's Business* 12, no. 2 (February 1921): 107–8 comes this: "Wanted—more mothers. We are short on homes; real homes. We are short on mothers; real mothers." J. Frank Norris called women who refused to have children "parasites on society" (Norris, "Home Foundation of All things, Says Rev. J. Frank Norris," *Searchlight* 2, no. 25 [22 April 1920]: 2). DeBerg, *Ungodly Women: Gender and the First Wave of American Fundamentalism* (Minneapolis: Augsburg/Fortress, 1990), 43–50.

20. Jesus' rebuke in Matthew 12:46–50 recasts motherhood and its importance in a woman's life. Women as well as men live in tension between ties to physical families and ties to the family of faith. Our physical family cannot be our primary focus. Our primary focus must be our relationship with God by faith and with others in that relationship. Motherhood is a good goal, but it must not be a first goal (Luke 14:26). The essence of discipleship is to know God as completely trustworthy and on that basis to do his will. The idolatry of motherhood can keep us from that.

21. Van Leeuwen, *Gender and Grace,* 176.

22. This was the central idea of Luke 10:25–37 as preached by Haddon Robinson, Heritage Baptist Church, Aurora, Colorado, 1980.

23. This book is about preaching to women, but the implications of what is written in this chapter must also be extended to men and women of different races and economic statuses.

Chapter 10

1. These six questions are adapted from Virginia Sapiro, *Women in American Society* (Palo Alto, Calif.: Mayfield Publishing, 1986), 287.

2. These characteristics reflect the lists in the Broverman chart in chapter 3.

3. Sapiro, *Women in American Society,* 287.

4. William D. Hendricks, *Exit Interviews* (Chicago: Moody Press, 1993), 261.

5. Ibid., 31.

6. Some preachers have found my book *A Woman God Can Lead: Lessons from Women of the Bible Help You Make Today's Choices* (Grand Rapids: Discovery House, 1998) helpful in preaching on the lives of women in the biblical narratives of the Old Testament and the Gospels.

Index